PRACTITIONER'S RESOURCE SERIES

SERIES EDITOR

Harold H. Smith, Jr., PhD
Smith, Sikorski-Smith, PA
Largo, Florida

CONSULTING EDITORS

William D. Anton, PhD
Director, Counseling and Wellness
University of South Florida
Tampa, Florida

Judith V. Becker, PhD
Professor of Clinical Psychology
Columbia University *and*
Director of Sexual Behavior Clinic
New York State Psychiatric Institute
New York, New York

Philip C. Boswell, PhD
Independent Practice in Clinical Psychology
Coral Gables, Florida

What Every Therapist Should Know About AIDS

Florence Kaslow, PhD
Director, Florida Couples and Family Institute
West Palm Beach, Florida

Peter A. Keller, PhD
Chair, Department of Psychology
Mansfield University
Mansfield, Pennsylvania

R. John Wakeman, PhD
Head, Department of Clinical Psychology
Ochsner Clinic and Ochsner Foundation Hospital
New Orleans, Louisiana

WHAT EVERY THERAPIST SHOULD KNOW ABOUT AIDS

Samuel Knapp, EdD
Harrisburg, Pennsylvania

Leon VandeCreek, PhD
Department of Psychology
Indiana University of Pennsylvania

Professional Resource Exchange, Inc.
Sarasota, Florida

Copyright © 1990 Professional Resource Exchange, Inc.
Professional Resource Exchange, Inc.
635 South Orange Avenue, Suites 4-6
Post Office Box 15560
Sarasota, FL 34277-1560

All rights reserved

No part of this book may be reproduced, stored in a retrieval system, or transmitted, in any form or by any means, either electronic, mechanical, photocopying, microfilming, recording, or otherwise, without written permission from the publisher.

Printed in the United States of America

Paperbound Edition ISBN: 0-943158-58-3
Library of Congress Catalog Number: 90-52652

The copy editor for this book was Patricia Hammond, the managing editor was Debbie Fink, the graphics coordinator was Laurie Girsch, and the cover designer was Bill Tabler.

SERIES PREFACE

As a publisher of books, cassettes, and continuing education programs, the Professional Resource Exchange strives to provide mental health professionals with highly applied resources that can be used to enhance clinical skills and expand practical knowledge.

All of the titles in the *Practitioner's Resource Series* are designed to provide important new information on topics of vital concern to psychologists, clinical social workers, marriage and family therapists, psychiatrists, and other mental health professionals.

Although the focus and content of each book in this series will be quite different, there will be notable similarities:

1. Each title in the series will address a timely topic of critical clinical importance.
2. The target audience for each title will be practicing mental health professionals. Our authors were chosen for their ability to provide concrete "how-to-do-it" guidance to colleagues who are trying to increase their competence in dealing with complex clinical problems.
3. The information provided in these books will represent "state-of-the-art" information and techniques derived from both clinical experience and empirical research. Each of these guide books will include references and

resources for those who wish to pursue more advanced study of the discussed topic.
4. The authors will provide numerous case studies, specific recommendations for practice, and the types of "nitty-gritty" details that clinicians need before they can incorporate new concepts and procedures into their practices.

We feel that one of the unique assets of the Professional Resource Exchange is that all of its editorial decisions are made by mental health professionals. The publisher, Larry Ritt, is a clinical psychologist and marriage and family therapist who maintains an active independent practice. The senior editor, Peter Keller, is a clinical psychologist who currently serves as chair of a psychology department and is actively involved in clinical training.

The editor of this series, Hal Smith, is a clinical psychologist in independent practice. He holds a diplomate in clinical psychology from the American Board of Professional Psychology, a diplomate in forensic psychology from the American Board of Forensic Psychology, and a diplomate in clinical neuropsychology from the American Board of Professional Neuropsychology. His specialties include clinical and forensic psychology, neuropsychology, stress management, management of chronic pain and psychophysiologic disorders, learning disabilities, interventions for spouse abusers, psychotherapy, psychodiagnostic evaluations, clinical hypnosis, and consultation.

We are also fortunate to have the services of an exceptionally well-qualified panel of consulting editors who assist in the selection and preparation of titles for this series: William D. Anton, Judith V. Becker, Philip C. Boswell, Florence Kaslow, and R. John Wakeman. Our consulting editors are all highly experienced clinicians. In addition, they have all made significant contributions to their professions as scholars, teachers, workshop leaders, researchers, and/or as authors and editors.

Lawrence G. Ritt, Publisher
Harold H. Smith, Jr., Series Editor

ABSTRACT

This book provides an overview of the major issues that every psychotherapist should be aware of concerning AIDS. As AIDS spreads, psychotherapists will be treating more patients with AIDS or relatives of persons with AIDS. Psychotherapists who treat patients with AIDS need to know about the psychosocial effects of AIDS on the patients and their families as well as basic information about the prevalence, modes of transmission, and methods of testing for AIDS. This knowledge base is especially important with cases of AIDS, an illness surrounded by myth and misinformation.

In addition, psychotherapists will be called upon to consult with organizations about their AIDS policies, and to develop, implement, or evaluate AIDS prevention programs. Because AIDS currently has no cure or vaccine, prevention and risk reduction programs are especially important. Fortunately, programs have been successfully conducted to encourage persons to change high risk sexual behavior. Other topics covered in this guide include pediatric AIDS, irrational fear of AIDS, staff discrimination against AIDS patients, and ethical issues in treating HIV positive patients.

TABLE OF CONTENTS

CONSULTING EDITORS	*iii*
SERIES PREFACE	*v*
ABSTRACT	*vii*
INTRODUCTION	1
AIDS AND HIV	2
Discovery of the HIV	2
Biology of AIDS	3
Stages of the Disease	4
EPIDEMIOLOGY	6
Distribution of AIDS Victims	7
Future Trends	9
HOW IS AIDS DIAGNOSED?	9
Pre-Test Counseling	10
Testing and Public Protection	10

What Every Therapist Should Know About AIDS

HOW IS AIDS TRANSMITTED?	11
Well-Documented Modes of Transmission	11
Direct Contact with Blood	11
Health Care Workers	12
Perinatal Transmission	12
Sexual Transmission	12
Condom Use	13
Variables in Transmission	14
Exposures to Multiple Partners	14
Presence of Other Sexually Transmitted Diseases	15
Patient Infectiousness	15
Vulnerability of the Immune System	16
Alternative Modes of Transmission	16
EDUCATIONAL INTERVENTIONS FOR CHANGING HIGH-RISK BEHAVIORS	17
School Education	17
Public Education Campaigns	19
Problems with Traditional Educational Campaigns	19
Effective Educational Programs	19
Population Targeted	20
Credibility of the Messenger	20
Concrete and Explicit Messages	21
Promoting Healthy Activities	22
Educational Programs Should Be Evaluated	22
A PROGRAM FOR REDUCING OR PREVENTING HIGH-RISK BEHAVIORS	23
Principles of Effective Behavior Change Programs	23
Educational Components	25
Cognitive Components	25
Behavioral Components	26
Affective Components	27
Environmental Components	28
Tailoring the Behavior Change Program	28
The Gay Lifestyle	28
Adolescents	29
Empirical Outcome of Behavior Change Programs	29

MENTAL HEALTH COUNSELING AND AIDS — 30

- Mental Health of AIDS Patients — 30
  - Life and Death Issues — 31
  - Depression — 32
  - Social Isolation and Social Support — 33
  - Neurological Disorders — 34
  - Suicide — 35
  - Dealing with Medical Personnel — 36
- Mental Health Needs of Friends and Family — 37
- Provider Issues — 38
  - Transference and Countertransference — 38
  - Reactions to Homosexuality — 39
  - Other Negative Feelings — 40
  - Overidentification — 40
  - Support Groups for Providers — 40

PEDIATRIC AIDS — 41

- Psychological and Neurological Issues — 41
- School Attendance Problems — 42
  - National Guidelines — 42

FEAR OF AIDS AS A CLINICAL SYMPTOM — 43

- Parallels with Syphilophobia — 43
- The Identification of AIDS Phobia — 44
  - The Worried Well — 44
  - The Pathoplastic AIDS Symptom — 45
- Predisposing Features of Patients Who Fear AIDS — 46
- Assessment of Patients Who Fear AIDS — 46
- Comments on Diagnostic Terminology — 48

STAFF REACTIONS TO AIDS — 48

- Combating Irrational Fears of Staff — 49

IS THERE A DUTY TO WARN IDENTIFIABLE POTENTIAL VICTIMS? — 50

- Ascertaining the Duty to Protect — 51
  - Fiduciary Relationship — 51
  - Identifiable Victim — 52

IS THERE A DUTY TO WARN IDENTIFIABLE POTENTIAL VICTIMS? *(Continued)*

Foreseeability	52
How to Ascertain Foreseeability	52
High-Risk Behaviors	53
Intermediate-Risk Behaviors	53
When HIV Status Is Unknown	54
Clinical Management of the HIV Dangerous Patient	54
Guidelines for Issuing Warnings	55
Potential Statutory Remedies	56

SUMMARY 57

REFERENCES 59

WHAT EVERY THERAPIST SHOULD KNOW ABOUT AIDS

INTRODUCTION

For the last 8 years, the Acquired Immunodeficiency Syndrome (AIDS) has spread rapidly throughout the homosexual and drug abusing populations of the United States. The spread is reminiscent of the spread of syphilis at the turn of the century. Although penicillin curtailed the syphilis epidemic, any such "magic bullet" that would prevent or cure AIDS appears to be decades away. Although the AIDS infection may have neared its high-water mark with the homosexual population, the extent of its spread into the heterosexual community remains to be seen.

The Centers for Disease Control (CDC) reported that in July, 1989, 105,000 Americans had acquired AIDS. The CDC projects that this number will increase to 270,000 persons by 1991. In addition, it is estimated that 1.5 to 2 million Americans will test positive for the Human Immunodeficiency Virus (HIV), the precursor for AIDS.

AIDS will eventually touch each of our lives. Psychotherapists will be treating more AIDS patients, as well as their friends and their relatives. Psychotherapists will also be called on to educate the public about AIDS and promote behavior change among the infected and noninfected populations. Psychotherapeutic skills are needed to reduce the social discrimination and fear of AIDS patients often found in schools, hospitals and other public institutions, and in families. In addition, some psychotherapy patients without AIDS will develop irrational fears and anxieties about AIDS transmission.

Cautious and informed concern is the optimal approach to AIDS. In order to treat AIDS patients and their families better, psychotherapists need to know the basic facts about AIDS, its prevalence, diagnosis, treatment, risk factors, and means to prevent its spread. Finally, psychotherapists need to know the common psychological and neurological symptoms that accompany AIDS, the social discrimination that AIDS patients face, and other special considerations when counseling persons with AIDS. This guide contains this essential information.

AIDS AND HIV

As recently as a decade ago, many scientists believed that the threat of infectious diseases in the developed world had been largely eliminated. Scientific attention focused on noninfectious conditions such as cancer and heart disease. This optimism over the management of infectious diseases ended with the identification of the HIV, an intracellular parasite, as the precursor of AIDS. The HIV is a special kind of virus called a retrovirus that had never before been identified as harmful to humans. Until the mid-1970s, many scientists believed that no infectious human retrovirus would ever be found.

DISCOVERY OF THE HIV

Researchers learned only in retrospect that the HIV began to spread in the United States in the middle 1970s. In the late 1970s, medical researchers in New York noted an increase in cases of Kaposi's Sarcoma (KS) among drug abusers. At the time, they speculated that certain drugs were contributing to this rare cancer which heretofore had been identified primarily in middle-aged Jewish or Italian males.

At about the same time, the CDC noted a sharp increase in requests for an experimental drug used only to treat the rare Pneumocystis Carinii Pneumonia (PCP). Further studies showed that the persons inflicted with KS or PCP were all male homosexuals or drug abusers suffering from a deficient immune system.

Interest increased as the number of patients with these infections grew. Largely due to the extraordinary discoveries of Robert Gallo of the United States and Luc Montagnier of France, a specific virus, now named the Human Immunodeficiency Virus (HIV), was identified as responsible for suppressing the immune system and allowing deadly cancers and infections to develop (Gallo & Montagnier, 1989).

Before the nomenclature was standardized, HIV was also called the human T-cell lymphotropic virus (HTLV-III), lymphadenopathy-associated virus (LAV), or AIDS associated retrovirus (ARV). HIV is now sometimes referred to as HIV-1 to distinguish it from HIV-2 which produces similar clinical syndromes but differs in structural properties. HIV-1 is prevalent throughout the world while HIV-2 co-exists with HIV-1 primarily in Africa. To date, HIV-2 strains have been very rare in the United States, but its spread in the United States is being monitored. The pathogenic quality of the HIV-2 is not as well established as that of HIV-1.

BIOLOGY OF AIDS

The following explanation of the infectious process is very simplified, but it should be sufficient for most psychotherapists. Retroviruses, like other viruses, cannot replicate on their own and must take over the biosynthetic apparatus of the host cell and exploit it for their own ends. The HIV infects the T-lymphocytes (also called T-4 cells), or the white blood cells that play a major role in the immune system's response to infection. The T-4 cells recognize foreign antigens or markers on infected cells and help to activate another set of white blood cells called B lymphocytes or B cells.

In a typical infection the B cells then multiply and produce specific antibodies that bind to infected cells and to other free organisms bearing the identified antigens. Mysteriously, the HIV slips into the helper T-cells and remains there permanently. Its elaborate genetic regulation enables it to remain safe from the surveillance of the immune system. While in the host cell, the HIV appears to derange the host cell's own genetic controls as it replicates slowly.

The HIV infects not only the T-4 cells but also another type of white blood cell, the macrophage. The macrophages are able to cross the blood-brain barrier and bring the virus into the brain, thus explaining the central nervous system pathology seen in many AIDS patients (Redfield & Burke, 1988).

Until the advent of recent treatments, the decline in the immune system was rapid. At least 30% of HIV-positive patients developed AIDS within 7 years of infection and another 40%

other clinical illnesses associated with HIV infection (Allen & Curran, 1988). One-third of AIDS patients die within 6 months of being diagnosed and 80% die within 2 years. Newer medical treatments can, however, extend the lives of persons with AIDS.

Death does not occur directly from the HIV. Rather, the impaired immune system allows cancers such as KS or opportunistic infections such as PCP to grow. Opportunistic infections are caused by agents that reside in healthy persons without causing diseases. These infections are not contagious.

The HIV replicates freely and appears in the fluid surrounding the brain and spinal cord, and in the blood. Fevers, rashes, flu-like symptoms, swollen glands, and sometimes neurological complaints often accompany the first stages of the HIV infection. Anywhere from 2 to 10 years after the first infection the immune system will have lost most of its T-4 cells and, as a result, it will fall prey to the pathogens that a healthy immune system could easily control (Redfield & Burke, 1988).

Prompt treatment can often prevent complications. For instance, medication given early in the course of the HIV infection can prevent PCP.

Although the HIV will always attack the immune system, cofactors influence the progression of the disease. AIDS may develop more quickly if the immune system is already weakened before the HIV infection. Stimulation of the immune system in response to later infections, such as the herpes virus, may also hasten disease progression. The herpes virus appears to interact with the HIV to increase the severity of HIV infection. Ordinarily, the human immune system can control the herpes simplex virus. When the HIV has impaired the immune system, however, the herpes virus may replicate freely and threaten health.

STAGES OF THE DISEASE

As the disease progresses, the patient moves through various stages, the last of which is AIDS. Table 1 on page 5 shows these stages.

The T-4 cell count initially increases in the first, acute stage of the infection. This acute stage can last anywhere from 6 weeks to 1 year after the initial infection. Most people have no symptoms during the first acute stage, although some will develop fatigue, fever, and swollen glands. In addition to these symptoms, which resemble those of mononucleosis, self-limited disorders of

TABLE 1: STAGES OF HIV INFECTION

	Exposure	HIV+	ARC	AIDS
	Asymptomatic			
Evidence of HIV Antibodies	No	Yes	Yes	Yes
Swollen Glands (Chronic Lymphadenopathy)	Maybe	No	Yes	Yes
Number of T-Helper Cells	> 400	< 400	< 400	< 100
Thrush (Mouth Sores)	No	No	Yes	Yes
Opportunistic Infections	No	No	No	Yes

the central nervous system have been noted ranging from headaches to encephalitis (inflammation of brain tissue).

Later the number of T-4 cells begins a slow decline. After the acute episode, the patient may be symptom free for a number of years. When the T-4 count drops below 400 (from a healthy average of 600), the person becomes abnormally vulnerable to infections. For the majority of people the first obvious sign of being infected is chronically swollen lymph nodes.

The second asymptomatic stage often lasts from 3 to 5 years while the patient still feels healthy. No one knows why the disease progresses so slowly, although it is possible that the immune system holds the infection in check for a while. This stage ends when the T-4 cell count persistently falls below 400. This is the harbinger of the decline in immune functioning. At this time, thrush, a fungal disease of the mouth, develops. This symptom is identified by a fungal infection of the mucous membranes of the tongue or mouth. It produces white spots or ulcers over the infected area. In addition, patients may develop herpes infections manifested by painful and persistent sores in the skin around the anus, the genital area, or the mouth. Also, many patients develop oral hairy leukoplakia, a mucous-membrane infection marked by fuzzy white patches on the tongue (Redfield & Burke, 1988).

Finally, because the HIV is neurotropic as well as lymphotropic, some patients will first show psychological signs of the infection. Patients may show apathy, emotional blunting, social withdrawal, or impaired thinking before overt physical signs develop.

In the third stage, infected persons may develop AIDS Related Complex (ARC) in which they have a number of AIDS symptoms such as fever, lymphadenopathy, and other symptoms, but do not manifest the opportunistic infections or cancers found in the "full-blown" AIDS syndrome.

In the last stage, patients have T-4 cell counts below 100 and are open to opportunistic infections. In addition, in many patients the virus has now crossed the blood-brain barrier with its host macrophage cells. Although the infection can cross the blood-brain barrier at any time after infection, the neurological damage is more likely to be severe and apparent at this stage. Early neurological findings include subtle alterations in cognitive functioning such as in memory and judgment. In the terminal stage, however, many patients develop AIDS dementia complex, a syndrome characterized by a gradual loss of precision in thought and motion. Eventually, some patients will be unable to walk or communicate effectively.

The dementia and wasting found in AIDS patients resembles the degeneration that may occur in aging persons. The continuing infections require numerous hospitalizations or home nursing. While nursing home care may be indicated, many facilities refuse to admit AIDS patients.

The HIV infection has two stages of increased infectiousness. First, people are likely to be highly infectious at the earliest stage of the infection before the immune system "kicks in" effectively. Also, they are more infectious in the later stages of the infection when the immune system has deteriorated.

EPIDEMIOLOGY

The data on the incidence and prevalence of AIDS is always changing and must be considered tentative, especially in third world countries. It is important to look at geographic variations because the spread of the infection varies with the frequency of high-risk factors such as intravenous contact with infected blood and sexual contact with infected persons.

AIDS has spread quite rapidly in the last 10 years. By December 1986, 28,000 Americans had acquired AIDS and by July, 1989, the figure had reached 105,000. During the last 4 years the number of verified cases of AIDS has been doubling every 18 months. The CDC estimates that the United States will have 270,000 cumulative cases of AIDS by 1991.

The number of worldwide cases of AIDS has doubled in the last 3 years. Despite this sharp increase, the number of identified cases under-represents the total number of persons with AIDS. Because underdeveloped countries do not have adequate resources for diagnosing or identifying AIDS, the real prevalence of the infection is probably double the number of diagnosed cases. Nevertheless, efforts are being made to increase the accuracy of these data.

About 1 million diagnosed cases of AIDS are expected throughout the world by 1991. The vast majority of AIDS cases in the next few years will involve people who are already infected.

Of course, the number of reported AIDS patients represents only the "tip of the iceberg." Exact prevalence of the HIV is difficult to determine because most patients are asymptomatic during the first years of infection. Persons can only learn if they have the infection through testing for HIV antibodies. Even the HIV testing can be misleading, however, because infected persons may not test seropositive until about 6 months after the infection, and some reports indicate a dormant period up to 3 years.

Instead, the prevalence of the infection must be extrapolated from the demographics of the persons already tested for the HIV. Nevertheless, the best estimates are that there are about 1 to 1.5 million infected persons in the United States and between 5 and 10 million persons worldwide (Board of Trustees, 1987). Most cases of AIDS that will develop in the next 5 years will be the product of the spread of the virus in the early 1980s before its deadly properties were identified and publicized.

DISTRIBUTION OF AIDS VICTIMS

The distribution of AIDS patients varies systematically according to geography and population demographics, depending on the frequency of high-risk behaviors.

What Every Therapist Should Know About AIDS

New York City has the highest prevalence of infection, followed by San Francisco, Los Angeles, Houston, Washington, DC, and Miami. In the United States the infection rate is higher in the Hispanic and Black populations where intravenous drug abuse is more common. Early reports showed that the percentage of AIDS victims was about twice as high in Black and Hispanic populations as among Caucasians. Later reports suggested that the extent of infection among Blacks and Hispanics was overestimated and that many more Caucasians had the disease than was previously believed. About 63% of adult cases have occurred in homosexual or bisexual men, 19% in heterosexual IV drug abusers, 7% in homosexual or bisexual IV drug abusers, 4% in hemophiliacs or other recipients of blood transfusions, and 4% in heterosexual men and women. The percentage of newly infected persons appears to be increasing for drug abusers and heterosexuals.

Beyond these general statistics, however, it may be better to consider AIDS as a series of subepidemics as opposed to one epidemic. In Western Europe, the United States, Latin America, and Australia the infection is spread primarily through IV drug abuse and homosexual behavior. Even in the U.S., however, the common mode of transmission differs among different populations. In California homosexuals account for 90% of the AIDS spread, while in New York City IV drug abusers account for 50% of the spread.

Heterosexual intercourse is the major cause of HIV transmission in Africa where the virus infects women almost as often as men. The reasons for this difference in the demographics of the infected population are unclear, but the greater incidence of venereal diseases, solicitation of prostitutes, or sharing of intravenous needles may spread the infection among heterosexuals in Africa (Quinn et al., 1986).

In addition, West Africa is the only common location for the HIV-2, a variation of the HIV-1 virus. To date, the HIV-2 coexists with HIV-1 in West Africa and has not spread rapidly.

The means of transmission with children differs from that of adults. Over three-fourths of the children with AIDS have been born to mothers with AIDS. Most of the rest acquired AIDS through blood transfusions. The number of children born with AIDS is likely to increase as the number of women with AIDS of child-bearing age increases. New cases of children acquiring AIDS through blood transmission are likely to be rare because the blood supply now is routinely checked for the HIV.

FUTURE TRENDS

The rate of the spread of the HIV has slowed in the United States. In part this is because the groups most likely to be infected through sexual behavior or IV drug abuse have already been infected. Furthermore, many persons have modified their high-risk sexual behaviors. Reports of decreases in syphilis within the gay community reflect this change in sexual behavior. Although the rate of increase has slowed, the absolute number of newly infected persons continues to grow, due to the greater number of persons who have the HIV.

Currently, AIDS is a major cause of mortality and morbidity within the United States. Due to the large number of persons who are already infected, the number of AIDS cases will increase over the next several years, especially where high-risk behaviors are common. The extent of increase will largely depend on the success of public health measures.

HOW IS AIDS DIAGNOSED?

AIDS is diagnosed through a combination of the enzyme-linked immunosorbent assay (ELISA) and the Western blot test. ELISA was first developed to test blood supplies and was later applied to individual patients. This simple and rapid blood test measures the presence of antibodies produced in reaction against HIV proteins, but the test has a high rate of "false positives" (blood samples falsely identified as HIV positive). The number of false positives is especially high among persons who have not engaged in high-risk behaviors such as sharing intravenous needles, participating in receptive anal sex, or having sexual relations with a partner known to test HIV positive. False negative test results are rare.

Supplementary or confirmatory tests distinguish between false positive and a true positive. Consequently, HIV testing should include a repeat of the ELISA. If the second ELISA is also positive, then the person should have the more expensive Western blot test. The diagnosis of HIV status should be made only if the patient tests positive on the Western blot test. There are other confirmatory tests, but at the present time the Western blot is considered the best for confirmation of the HIV infection (Consortium for Retrovirus Serology Standardization, 1988).

Because the antibodies for the HIV may not appear for several months to perhaps 3 years after infection, the tests may not accurately identify the disease in recently infected persons. Persons who engage in high-risk behaviors should be retested periodically.

Unfortunately, many hospitals routinely screen for HIV without providing this information about false positives to patients. Only 58% of American hospitals with infectious disease training programs provided counseling with the AIDS testing (Henry, Willenbring, & Crossley, 1988). As a result, many persons from low-risk groups who have taken a single ELISA have undergone unnecessary emotional trauma caused by the belief that they had AIDS.

PRE-TEST COUNSELING

Pre-test counseling is indicated for all persons who take the ELISA or other tests for HIV. The counseling should explain the meaning of the test and its limitations, including factual information about false positives, false negatives, and the incubation period. In addition, the counseling should help patients anticipate their reactions to the test results. Patients currently engaging in high-risk behaviors should be encouraged to change their lifestyles.

Test takers should also consider whom to inform if they are HIV positive. Pre-test counselors encourage test takers to share the knowledge with sexual partners and their family doctor and dentist. The pre-test counseling is so important that many experts discourage the use of home-based tests.

TESTING AND PUBLIC PROTECTION

Statistics about the prevalence of AIDS and the testing for HIV are being used to track the course of the AIDS epidemic. Currently all states and the District of Columbia require physicians to report cases of AIDS. The definition of AIDS follows a strict case definition developed by the CDC in order to promote consistency in reporting. As of 1987, nine states (Arizona, Colorado, Idaho, Kentucky, Minnesota, Mississippi, Montana, South Carolina, and Wisconsin) also required the reporting of positive HIV status (Curran, Clark, & Gostin, 1987).

All states have voluntary "partner notification" programs that could help reduce the spread of the disease. Partner notification programs have been in existence as part of the program to control other sexually transmitted diseases for years. In these voluntary programs, the infected person or a service provider for the infected person (with the patient's consent) seeks help in informing a partner of the infection. Trained health department personnel can instruct patients about how to inform their partners with sensitivity. Reports of the outcome with partner notification programs have been positive ("Partner Notification," 1988).

Recently, some writers have referred to partner notification programs as "contact tracing" programs. This may lead to some confusion since "contact tracing" once referred to involuntary partner identification programs that were used to control other venereal diseases. Such involuntary programs are not currently used to control the HIV epidemic.

HOW IS AIDS TRANSMITTED?

The likely means of transmission of AIDS were identified before the etiological agent was identified. It is well established that AIDS transmission occurs primarily through three means: semen, blood, and birth.

WELL-DOCUMENTED MODES OF TRANSMISSION

AIDS is transmitted through the direct contact of blood such as through blood transfusions or intravenous blood contact, from mother to child, and through sexual contact, especially receptive anal intercourse. Vaginal intercourse is also a potential source of infection, although in the United States it is not a primary source at this time. In addition to these well-documented risk factors, isolated reports have been cited of alternative modes of transmission that will be discussed below.

Direct Contact with Blood. At one time hemophiliacs were at high risk to contact AIDS because of contaminated blood supplies. In recent years, serological methods to screen blood for HIV and screening of donors have cleaned the blood supply, and AIDS transmission through blood transfusions now is very unlikely. Although the future rate of infection from the blood supply is minimal, many patients have already been infected and the number of diagnosed blood-donated AIDS cases will continue to rise. Hemophiliacs represent about 1% of all American AIDS cases (Heyward & Curran, 1988).

The shared use of intravenous needles, syringes, and other drug abuse paraphernalia accounts for a large and increasing percentage of the cases of HIV infection. Intravenous drug abusers account for most of the spread of the epidemic in the East Coast, in contrast to the West Coast where spread through homosexual behavior is more common.

Health Care Workers. Health care workers have a low risk of acquiring the HIV infection from contact with blood. Nevertheless, several health care workers have tested positive after exposure of abraded skin or mucous membranes to infected blood. Of 963 exposures of health care workers, only four were positive in testing 6 months after the exposure. The occupational risk of acquiring HIV in health care settings is most often associated with percutaneous inoculation of blood from a patient with HIV infection. Even then, the risk of infection following needlestick exposures to blood from HIV-infected patients is less than 1% (Gerbert et al., 1988).

Perinatal Transmission. The transmission of HIV from mother to fetus in utero occurs in about 40% to 50% of pregnancies of HIV-positive mothers (Allen & Curran, 1988). In addition, transmissions have occurred through the exchange of blood during delivery or through breast feeding. For this reason, the CDC recommends that HIV-positive mothers not breast feed their children.

Sexual Transmission. HIV transmission also occurs through sexual acts. AIDS spreads rapidly among the homosexual population because of the frequency of anal sex among that group. Homosexual men who engage in anal sex are likely to have higher rates of AIDS than homosexual men who do not. Other sexual acts commonly performed by homosexuals, such as fisting, also increase the risk of transmission.

Nevertheless, HIV transmission is caused by sexual practice, not sexual orientation. The mere fact of being gay does not predispose a person to HIV infection; only the sexual acts commonly found in the gay lifestyle increase the risk of infection.

Anal sex is a major mode of transmission of AIDS among heterosexuals also. Women who engage in anal intercourse, especially unprotected anal intercourse, place themselves at a greater risk than women who do not practice anal intercourse (Bolling & Voeller, 1987). Because men are not passive recipients of anal sexual intercourse from women, the rate of infection from women to men is lower than from men to women.

The HIV infection can also be transmitted through vaginal intercourse (Friedland & Klein, 1987; Padian et al., 1987). The HIV is found both in semen and in the genital secretions of women with the infection. Vaginal intercourse, however, is not now one of the common modes of transmission. Transmission through fellatio is rare, but has been reported.

Infection through sexual behavior occurs when semen or vaginal secretions make contact with open wounds. Such wounds are likely to occur during anal intercourse. They are less likely to occur through vaginal intercourse or fellatio, although it is possible for a sexual partner to have microscopic lesions.

Some experts have predicted that the rate of heterosexual transmission will increase in the United States (Friedland & Klein, 1987). The proportion of AIDS cases attributable to heterosexual contact increased from about 1% in 1982 to 4% in 1989 and is projected to reach at least 5% by 1991 (Chamberland & Dondero, 1987).

Condom Use. The conscientious use of undamaged condoms, especially when used in conjunction with spermicides such as nonoxynol-9, can greatly reduce the frequency of anal or vaginal transmission. Hearst and Hulley (1988) have developed estimated risks of infection with or without condoms. Using condoms there is a 1 in 5,000 risk of acquiring the HIV infection on the basis of one sexual encounter, and a 1 in 11 risk on the basis of 500 sexual encounters. Without using condoms there is a 1 in 500 risk of acquiring the HIV infection on the basis of 1 sexual encounter and a 1 in 3 risk on the basis of 500 sexual encounters. Although condoms can greatly reduce transmission, they are not infallible. Of course, as the infection spreads, the risk with each different sexual partner will increase.

The effective use of condoms for AIDS prevention differs from that for pregnancy prevention. Condoms or spermicide must be used at every sexual encounter to prevent HIV transmission whether or not one of the partners is temporarily sterile due to menstruation or other reasons. Condoms must also be used during anal intercourse.

In reality, however, condom use is a complicated behavior governed by many social variables, and not just by the knowledge of infectious status. The efficacy of condoms in the laboratory does not necessarily translate into effective use in actual practice. User failure is common, and incomplete compliance is also common.

Latex condoms only should be used and oil-based lubricants should be avoided because they quickly destroy the latex. Users should open the package properly so as not to tear the condom, should roll the condom to the base of the penis to avoid loss of semen, and should allow a space for air at the tip of the condom to collect the semen. Finally, users should withdraw soon after ejaculation and hold the condom at the base of the penis when withdrawing. *Consumer Reports* has reported recently on shortcomings and advantages of different brands of condoms ("Can You Rely on Condoms," 1989).

Evidence shows that the use of condoms can greatly reduce risk of transmission. Consequently, the CDC (1988a) promotes condom use.

> Recommendations for prevention of STD [Sexually Transmitted Disease], including HIV infection, should emphasize that risk of infection is most effectively reduced through abstinence or sexual intercourse with a mutually faithful uninfected partner. Condoms do not provide absolute protection from any infection, but if properly used, they should reduce the risk of infection. (p. 1927)

In addition to their benefit in reducing the risk of HIV transmission, condoms also reduce the risk of other STDs which appear to increase the risk of transmission of the HIV.

Variables in Transmission. Despite what is known about the transmission of AIDS, the risk of infection varies considerably. Several possible factors under study at this time are the presence of other STDs, the degree of infectiousness of the host, and the vulnerability of the receptive partner (Chamberland & Dondero, 1987).

Exposures to Multiple Partners. The number of sexual partners increases proportionately the risk of developing AIDS. Despite publicity about sexual activity within the United States, 80% of Americans have had either none or one sexual partner in the last year, which puts them at a low risk of developing AIDS. Nevertheless, many Americans do have multiple sexual partners and are at risk of having sexual relations with a person who has AIDS ("Number of Sexual Partners," 1988).

Presence of Other Sexually Transmitted Diseases. The presence of other STDs may increase the likelihood of transmitting or receiving AIDS. HIV infection is associated with genital ulcerative diseases, syphilis and herpes simplex virus (Stamm et al., 1988).

Skin lesions, such as those frequently found in the early stage of syphilis, can provide the portal of entry needed for the HIV to reach the lymph or blood circulatory system. The high rate of STDs in African countries may partially explain the rate of heterosexual infection there (Potterat, 1987). Of course the presence of STDs only increases the likelihood of developing AIDS through vaginal intercourse. The HIV can still be transmitted through vaginal intercourse even in the absence of another STD.

The prevalence of STDs may help explain differences in the geographic distribution of HIV infection and in its relationship to sexual orientation. The prevalence and severity of STDs may be substantially lower among North American heterosexuals than among North American homosexuals, or central African prostitutes and their customers. This may explain the similarity in the epidemiologic characteristics of the HIV infection in North American homosexual men and African heterosexuals.

This information has important implications for the containment of the disease. The early diagnosis and treatment of syphilis and comprehensive contact investigation might reduce the spread of the HIV. In addition, educating persons with other STDs may help control HIV spread.

Patient Infectiousness. HIV hosts vary in their infectiousness. It has been suggested that some persons transmit the virus more efficiently than others and that infectiousness may vary over the course of the infection. As the immune system of the HIV infected person weakens, it is claimed, the HIV replicates more rapidly and is more prevalent in body fluids, so that sexual partners are more likely to be infected (Osmond et al., 1988).

This theory is supported by the fact that scientists can isolate more HIVs as the number of T-helper cells declines and the clinical course of the disease progresses. If this theory is true, then physicians should eventually be able to identify the degree of infectiousness with more precision. Unfortunately, this would also mean that the overall rate of HIV transmission will accelerate as the disease progresses within the recently infected population.

Vulnerability of the Immune System. Finally, some believe that the overall health and immune system of uninfected persons influence their vulnerability to the HIV. As noted above, the concurrent infection with herpes simplex may weaken the immune system and make the person more vulnerable to infection. The abuse of recreational drugs or alcohol and increased levels of stress appear to weaken the immune system and increase receptivity to the HIV.

ALTERNATIVE MODES OF TRANSMISSION

Isolated reports have been made of alternative ways of transmitting the HIV such as through casual social contact. Unverified reports have also been made of transmission through human bites. At the same time, several known instances of human bites by HIV-infected persons have not resulted in infection. Reports of transmission through kissing or tattoos have not yet been verified (Castro et al., 1988). Transmission has not been documented through normal social contact or through food, tears, urine, or exposure to toilet seats, drinking glasses, doorknobs, shower stalls, sneezes, coughs, saliva, sweat, insect bites, or food prepared by an HIV positive person (Friedland & Klein, 1987).

Fear about casual transmission may have arisen because HIV has been found in saliva and tears, although the isolation rate was much lower than in blood. Part of the reason for the difficulty of casual transmission is that the virus is fragile outside of the human body. HIV deactivates when exposed to heat or common household detergents and cleansers. In addition, large doses of the virus are often necessary to successfully infect another person.

Fischl et al. (1987) showed that persons in daily contact with the victims are at no risk of developing AIDS. These researchers followed the families of 45 adults with AIDS, including 45 spouses, 109 children, and 29 adult household members aside from spouses. All had close contact with the infected patient, including sharing kitchen and bathroom facilities, and hugging and kissing. None of the casual adult household members who were not spouses of the victims contracted AIDS. None of the children without high-risk activity seroconverted.

In contrast, spouses of the infected patient often acquired the disease, apparently through sexual intercourse. About half the infected couples engaged in only vaginal intercourse. Couples who abstained from sexual intercourse did not transmit the disease. Only 1 out of 10 spouses who used condoms seroconverted, a rate roughly consistent with the predictions of Hearst and Hulley (1988). Out of 14 spouses who did not use condoms 12 seroconverted.

Reports of casual transmission often result in unnecessary panic and unwarranted social restrictions on HIV carriers. In reality, the modes of transmission have been stable throughout the course of the disease.

EDUCATIONAL INTERVENTIONS FOR CHANGING HIGH-RISK BEHAVIORS

No vaccine or cure for AIDS is forthcoming in the near future, and behavior change is the only way to slow the spread of the infection. The first step in a behavior change program is to accurately inform the public about AIDS. Toward this end, educational campaigns are crucial, but successful educational campaigns require considerable sophistication. Furthermore, even campaigns that are successful in disseminating accurate information are usually not sufficient to lead to actual behavior change. Instead, the behavior change may require participation in intense psychologically based groups.

This section will discuss the ingredients of educational campaigns designed to disseminate accurate information. Later, we will present the elements of successful behavior change programs.

The CDC (1988b) views public education as a long-term commitment. Because of the urgency of the AIDS epidemic, however, the CDC has encouraged the dissemination of programs to change sexual behavior even before going through the usual process of evaluation for effectiveness. Early research indicates that such programs can be effective.

SCHOOL EDUCATION

Many Americans have incorrect beliefs about AIDS despite widespread educational efforts by the government and private sources. Almost 10% of high school students believed that AIDS could be transmitted by shaking hands, 40% by contact in public toilets, 50% by giving blood, and 60% by insect bites. Data on misinformation held by adults is not available, but anecdotal reports suggest that it is also high ("HIV-Related Beliefs," 1988).

The CDC has issued broad guidelines for school-based educational programs on AIDS, although they recommend that programs involve community input. These guidelines recommend education appropriate to the emotional and developmental level of students. The CDC also recommends that education address specific needs of minorities such as making the information available in languages other than English.

Within the school system, the lessons about AIDS are intended to be cumulative. That is, the information given in elementary school is a basis for later information. Community groups should establish the age at which the students receive this information by considering the normative behavior within the community.

A major goal of AIDS education is to thwart "AIDS hysteria." The CDC recommends that elementary school teachers emphasize that AIDS is hard to get and, while it causes some people to get very sick, does not commonly affect children. Also, children should be taught that scientists all over the world are working hard to find a cure or vaccine and that children can avoid the infection.

In later elementary school years children can be taught basic information about the viral cause of the disease and the way it attacks the immune system. They can also be taught that people can contract AIDS by sexual contact, sharing needles, and by birth if the mother has AIDS.

In junior and senior high school, the curriculum can be more adult oriented. The goal is to prevent adolescents from engaging in high-risk behaviors. The programs should encourage students to abstain from high-risk behaviors such as unprotected sexual intercourse (unless in a mutually monogamous relationship) and IV drug abuse.

A significant number of teenagers engage in high-risk behaviors. Approximately 2.5 million teenagers are infected with STDs each year and about 1% of teenagers abuse IV drugs.

Recognizing the shortcomings of "passive education," the CDC recommends that schools discuss preventive behaviors such as encouraging students having intercourse to use latex condoms, avoiding sexual relationships with anyone who may be infected, seeking treatment if using illegal drugs, and seeking HIV counseling and testing if HIV infection is suspected.

These safe practice suggestions are the most controversial of the CDC's recommendations. Some community leaders believe that teaching children about "safer sex" practices condones or encourages them to engage in sex, or that discussions about cleaning needles condones drug abuse. Others disagree and believe that some teenagers are going to engage in high-risk activities anyway and that they should understand how to reduce their risks.

DiClemente (1989) believes that high school education programs should go beyond just teaching facts about AIDS. "Knowledge is necessary, but not sufficient to promote behavior change among adolescents without incorporating other health education strategies" (p. 75). DiClemente recommends peer-directed discussions, support groups, "resistance thinking," and role playing of potentially high-risk situations.

PUBLIC EDUCATION CAMPAIGNS

The CDC has been a leader in educational programs and has taken several steps to educate the public such as sending an informational brochure to every U.S. household, developing a national AIDS information toll-free hot line, and producing a clearinghouse system that will maintain a comprehensive inventory of AIDS information, resources, and services. Psychotherapists can utilize all of these resources in educating their patients.

Problems with Traditional Educational Campaigns. The government sponsors many of these educational programs through the public media, but the failure of informational campaigns alone to change behavior is well-documented. During the syphilis epidemics in the early part of this century, for example, the American government launched very extensive public information campaigns to get soldiers and civilians to change their sexual habits. These programs emphasized the means of transmission and negative consequences of syphilis infection. They were, however, unable to stop the spread of syphilis (Brandt, 1988).

Initial public information campaigns about AIDS have had similar results. Although gay men in general have shown decreases in the frequency of unprotected anal intercourse, number of sexual partners, and an increased use of condoms during anal intercourse, many individuals still engage in high-risk sexual behaviors (Becker & Joseph, 1988).

Effective Educational Programs. It is now realized that effective educational programs need to be carefully constructed.

They must take into account the unique aspects of the targeted group, have a credible source, give concrete and explicit information, promote positive attitudes towards healthy activities, and be capable of being evaluated.

Population Targeted. As noted earlier, AIDS is best considered as a series of "subepidemics" as opposed to one epidemic (Valdiserri, 1988). For example, risk-reduction messages produced for middle-class gay men are not appropriate for inner city drug abusing youth. The educational program must reflect the special characteristics and needs of the target group.

Educational programs often fail because they do not target the population carefully. One of the most common problems is ignorance about the language and cultural nuances of the targeted population. Materials designed for middle-class teenagers would differ from those designed for homosexual adults and from those targeted towards linguistic or racial minorities.

It is not enough that the materials be produced in Spanish, Black English, and so on. The culture of the audience must be considered. It is erroneous, for example, to speak of Hispanic populations as if they were homogeneous. The cultural differences between a New York Puerto Rican, a Miami Cuban, and a Los Angeles second generation Mexican can be quite substantial.

Culturally appropriate materials can appeal to dominant values of the subgroup. "Machismo" is believed to be common among Hispanic males and involves male dominance and a pride in male characteristics. An AIDS educational campaign can appeal to "Machismo" by pointing out that sexually cautious males are fulfilling their "manly" functions of protecting their family from illness.

An AIDS educational campaign can appeal to the gay community by including safer sex habits as aspects of "gay pride" or "gay solidarity." In the first stages of the AIDS epidemic, the government urged persons to use condoms more and to reduce the frequency of anal sex, but the gay community did not view that as being necessary or desirable. Gradually, gay leaders are helping to create a new social norm wherein sexual responsibility is a desirable feature in the gay community.

Credibility of the Messenger. Another feature that limited the effectiveness of traditional campaigns was that the source of information did not have credibility in the target audience. Often minority groups feel suspicious about official proclamations. Be-

What Every Therapist Should Know About AIDS

cause of social discrimination against groups who engage in high-risk behaviors, messages must overcome suspiciousness about the "authorities." At first many gays believed that government publicity about AIDS was part of an anti-gay morality campaign that exploited and exaggerated the fear of AIDS to discourage homosexual behavior. Others believed that the government fabricated statistics describing the increase of AIDS.

Culturally appropriate education can be especially successful if indigenous leaders work in cooperation with public health leaders. Successful programs have included, for example, a bilingual theater group for teenagers, and skating parties and music festivals interspersed with "pep talks" on sexual responsibility. Other interventions have included making dance videos with AIDS messages, or teaching prostitutes to teach other prostitutes to use condoms.

These innovative educational programs were developed because of the limitations of pamphlets or public service announcements. Even well designed pamphlets have an intrinsic limitation because the intended reader may not be motivated to read it carefully. Grassroots educational programs that involve interesting messages or direct personal contact tend to do better.

Indigenous educational campaigns have several advantages. Indigenous workers allow the government to target highly specific populations where the incidence of AIDS or other STDs may be high. These local "authorities" have greater credibility than public officials, and they can take advantage of existing social networks to support their work. Indigenous workers can help mold a cultural milieu that accepts or expects safe behavior. For example, these workers can promote positive behaviors such as participation in gay advocacy groups, religious groups, or gay service groups as one way to affirm "gayness," while not encouraging high-risk sexual activity.

Concrete and Explicit Messages. The topic of explicit educational materials is closely aligned to the cultural sensitivity of the materials. Materials that talk about the need to avoid "exchanging bodily fluids" may mean little to certain audiences, whereas explicit street language may convey the meaning accurately. The street language may, however, offend a middle-class audience which may oppose its distribution.

The emphasis on "safer sex" or "clean needles" comes from the recognition that many pleasurable high-risk behaviors are hard to change. Often changing these behaviors requires intensive psychologically based programs such as are described later (see also Kelly & St. Lawrence, 1988). The motives of health related behavior must be addressed if the behavior is to be modified. Preliminary results with these programs suggest that modification is possible and that long-term changes can occur.

Promoting Healthy Activities. Although educational programs cannot replace intense psychologically based programs, the educational programs supplement or support the content of the psychological programs. "Playing it safe" messages can be followed by positive messages on the benefits of a safer lifestyle, such as freedom from fear, positive health, secure and stable relationships, and positive self-esteem.

Much of the original AIDS education focused on fear and the dire consequences of contracting an HIV infection. The fear motive was clear in the name of Australia's public information campaign: the "Grim Reaper" campaign. Public campaigns based only on fear may make some people too discouraged to reform their behavior, and may lead to anti-gay hysteria or AIDS-phobia.

The emphasis on healthy activities can refer to psychologically healthy as well as physically healthy activities. Participation in constructive ethnic or gay groups can fulfill psychological needs, give social supports, and provide access to up-to-date and accurate information.

Educational Programs Should Be Evaluated. As noted above, the urgency of the AIDS epidemic has led to the development of educational campaigns even before their effectiveness was verified. Despite the reasonableness of the CDC's approach, it is desirable to conduct some evaluation of these educational programs *post hoc.*

Evaluation of these programs is difficult because of the long latency between the target behavior (reduction of high-risk behavior) and the ultimate goal of reducing the spread of AIDS. Nevertheless, certain intermediate dependent variables may be useful to estimate the success of these programs. The self-reported amount of high-risk activities, incidence of other STDs such as gonorrhea or syphilis, records of sale of condoms in high-risk communities, and number of persons requesting testing may be used as dependent variables.

Currently, educational programs are being evaluated to determine which types are the most effective. Nevertheless, experience with past public health improvement campaigns suggests that effective programs should include the elements discussed previously: They should consider the unique aspects of the targeted group, give concrete and specific information, promote positive attitudes toward healthy activities, and be capable of being evaluated.

A PROGRAM FOR REDUCING OR PREVENTING HIGH-RISK BEHAVIORS

In this section we present a multifaceted program applicable to most persons who desire to change their high-risk behaviors. Although accurate information is a necessary step, it does not automatically lead to behavior change. For example, people who choose celibacy may occasionally lose their resolve and engage in binges of high-risk behavior. Problems with adherence are especially problematic for highly pleasurable activities such as sexual intercourse or drug abuse. This problem is similar to that observed in treatment of overeating or smoking. Nevertheless, evidence suggests that a combined educational and psychological format can produce high and consistent levels of change.

PRINCIPLES OF EFFECTIVE BEHAVIOR CHANGE PROGRAMS

The basic program can be used for HIV-negative persons who do not currently engage in high-risk behavior (such as adolescents who are at the age when experimentation in high-risk behavior begins). It can also be used with persons for whom sexual behavior is problematic, such as HIV-negative persons who engage in high-risk behavior or any HIV-positive person.

Although this behavior change format has certain common features for all groups, the psychotherapist should alter the basic format to account for differences among the targeted groups. It is highly desirable to involve representatives from the target community in all phases of the program. Effective behavior change programs must also take into account the vernacular and peer group references of the targeted audience. The common language can be more readily understood and is more acceptable because it is less likely to appear imposed from government or health authorities.

Table 2 (p. 24) shows the ingredients of this program. This program is comprehensive and theoretically sound. Like most other behavior change programs, however, it has not been tested

TABLE 2: CRUCIAL INGREDIENTS OF BEHAVIOR CHANGE

EDUCATIONAL:

1. Facts about AIDS
2. Misconceptions
3. Facts about behavior change

COGNITIVE:

1. Self-talk (identifying and modifying dysfunctional beliefs related to high-risk behaviors)
2. Thought-stopping

BEHAVIOR - SOCIAL SKILLS TRAINING:

1. Sexual assertiveness
2. Relationship enhancement

    a. Soliciting emotional support
    b. Expressing emotions
    c. Listening skills

AFFECTIVE:

1. Identifying dysfunctional emotions related to high-risk behavior: disappointment, frustration, rejection, excitement
2. Identifying positive emotions related to safe behavior: increased intimacy, self-esteem, self-control

ENVIRONMENTAL:

1. Situational triggers to high-risk behavior: alcohol, certain bars, certain people
2. Cognitive triggers: fear of disapproval
3. Emotional triggers: frustration, anxiety, loneliness

empirically. It relies heavily upon the work of Valdiserri et al. (1987) and Kelly and St. Lawrence (1988) who have reported an initial high degree of success. Because of the urgency in changing behavior, the CDC has encouraged the development and implementation of these programs immediately, and anticipates that they will be refined later.

This program could be called a multifaceted program that intervenes on the educational, cognitive, behavioral, affective, and environmental levels. We believe this multifaceted approach has the best chance of producing behavior change.

The group format is important because peer pressure and group norms are important factors in reinforcing appropriate behavior. Often the group members become friends after the termination of the group and can use each other for support, as do members of Alcoholics Anonymous or Recovery Incorporated.

Educational Components. Accurate information is a necessary first step in any comprehensive program for behavior change. Not only must the program teach the basic facts about AIDS, but participants must also unlearn misconceptions about AIDS. Teenagers are particularly ignorant about AIDS or sex in general. For other groups personal involvement in high-risk behaviors may lead to selective perception about the facts of AIDS. They may minimize the hazards of transmission through their preferred modes of sexual activity.

The suggested content for an educational program involves information on transmission, incubation, spectrum of diseases related to the HIV infection, risks of specific sexual practices, information about tests, and proper use of condoms.

In order to be effective, these educational materials need to acknowledge that some groups will be engaging in behavior that is not universally accepted, such as homosexual acts or abuse of intravenous drugs. No one disputes that AIDS prevention programs should include information on the benefits of monogamy or abstinence. But educational materials will not be effective if they fail to provide information on safer sex techniques for those who continue in nonmonogamous relationships. Most of the appropriate educational information has been covered in earlier portions of this guide.

Cognitive Components. The cognitive component addresses the dysfunctional beliefs that interfere with the implementation of effective behavior change. Statements of some of these common beliefs, derived from AIDS-specific applications of Rational Emotive Therapy (RET) principles (Ellis & Harper 1975), are listed in Table 3.

Denial is a common cognitive defense mechanism that pervades these beliefs. Group members learn to recognize the irrationality of such ideas and to dispute them when they arise. The training here includes group efforts such as modeling and teaching each other. This increases understanding of the principles and helps create a group atmosphere where functional beliefs are more acceptable.

Behavioral Components. The behavioral component emphasizes social-skills training including assertiveness (e.g., Alberti & Emmons, 1978) and relationship enhancement (Guerney, 1977). Group participants are given assertiveness training for sexual interactions, learning, for example, how to refuse unwanted sexual advances and how to express a desire for the use of safer sex or noncoital relationships.

The behavioral component also emphasizes relationship-building skills. Often people seek multiple sexual adventures because they do not know how to participate in a single relationship over time. Learning how to improve relationships should

---

TABLE 3: DYSFUNCTIONAL BELIEFS RELATED TO AIDS

---

1. It is better to engage in high-risk behavior than to lose the approval of persons I consider important.
2. Because I have failed once at changing high-risk behaviors, I will always fail.
3. Eliminating high-risk behavior means losing all pleasurable activities.
4. I do not have the ability to control my emotions and the outlets of my sexual energies.
5. I am a healthy person and will not get AIDS despite engaging in high-risk behavior.
6. I can always tell who is HIV infected and can avoid high-risk behavior with them.

---

reduce the likelihood of seeking multiple sexual partners. Training can be provided in expressive and empathic modes of conversation, in the ability to express perceptions, thoughts, and feelings in an acceptable manner, and in being able to listen to the partner's expression of the same in an understanding manner (Guerney, 1977).

As with cognitive skills, it is important to practice these communication skills. Situations can be enacted realistically using the street vernacular and credible confrontations and scenarios.

Communication skills are also important for continuing safer sex behaviors in an existing relationship. Often partners will discontinue condom use after a relationship is "stable" for several months or weeks. Persons infatuated with a new partner may be reluctant to show "distrust" by insisting upon safer sex practices for a longer period of time. Nevertheless, some sexually active persons may, in honest ignorance, acquire an infection. Anecdotal reports from prostitutes indicate that many HIV infected prostitutes conscientiously use condoms with their partners, but not with their boyfriends who infect them.

Affective Components. The affective component includes identification of both negative and positive emotions. Often participants will have resentment, disappointment, frustration, or grief related to the development of the AIDS epidemic. In addition, participants can identify and express positive emotions that have developed out of the acquisition of their new cognitive and behavioral skills. These positive emotions can be associated with an increased capacity for intimacy in close relationships, self-esteem at being assertive, and sexual and emotional self-control.

The affective component also includes consideration of how unmet emotional needs often cause undesired sexual behavior. The optimal program should then address these emotional issues rather than merely attempt to reduce or eliminate risky sexual behaviors. Quadland and Shattls (1987) claim that loneliness, a sense of inadequacy, and anxiety (not just the need for genital gratification) cause much ego-dystonic sexual behavior. Persons can use sex as a diversion from their social and emotional needs.

> It is important to recognize that freedom of sexual expression is accomplished when individuals are not oppressed by their own, as well as society's perceived needs, but rather when they are free to make choices about their sexual lives. (p. 293)

The overlap between program components is obvious. The expression of emotion may utilize many behavioral skills. The identification of unmet psychological needs which result in loneliness, inadequacy, or anxiety overlaps considerably with the development of cognitive awareness or insight.

Environmental Components. Finally, the environmental precipitants of high-risk behaviors need to be identified. Often external situational factors such as consuming alcohol, going to bars, or being around certain people can trigger high-risk behaviors. Other situational factors are cognitive or emotional. For example, disappointment at past failures to control behavior or fear of disapproval may trigger high-risk episodes. Emotional triggers may include frustration, anxiety, or loneliness.

After identifying the environmental precipitants, group members can practice ways to reduce these problems. Some situational precipitants, like certain bars or drinking alcohol, can be avoided or eliminated. Assertive behaviors can be strengthened to counter unwanted sexual advances or intrusions. Unpleasant emotions can be expressed to a loved one instead of being denied or diverted into sexual behavior. Unproductive cognitions can be challenged and replaced with more productive thoughts.

TAILORING THE BEHAVIOR CHANGE PROGRAM

Psychotherapists have been cautioned against the "uniformity myth" when selecting psychotherapy treatments for patients. Similarly, they must also be cautioned against a "uniformity myth" when it comes to behavioral self-control.

The Gay Lifestyle. Programs targeted toward gay men need to focus on the unique aspects of gay sexual relationships. Sexual activity is a predominant feature for some participants in the gay lifestyle and is associated with more than just genital gratification. Instead, it is used as a social vehicle to reduce anxiety, overcome loneliness, or establish a "macho" image.

Many gay couples do not have an extensive social support system. They may not be invited to parties or social gatherings as heterosexual couples would be. Consequently, there is more pressure on the gay intimate relationship to fill more of the couple's needs.

In addition, some gay men may focus so extensively on their sexuality that they have not learned other skills that are necessary for developing and maintaining intimate relationships, such as conflict resolution, self-discipline, or empathic listening.

Psychotherapists need to avail themselves of a wide repertoire of means to promote safe or safer behaviors, including resources from the gay community. For example, the identification of a speaker as being "gay affirmative" may give him or her credibility beyond the content or reasoning of the speech. Psychotherapists should encourage patients to attend lectures or support groups for HIV-positive persons that are led by respected gay leaders.

Adolescents. In 1988 adolescents (persons aged 13 to 21) constituted only about 2% of the total population infected with AIDS, but this incidence was double what it was 1 year earlier. The need for prevention among adolescents is imperative. About 20% of the persons infected with AIDS are in their 20s, which means that most of them acquired the infection through behaviors in their teens. Consequently, it is important that adolescents learn good judgment and responsibility before they start becoming sexually active or involved with intravenous drugs.

EMPIRICAL OUTCOME OF
BEHAVIOR CHANGE PROGRAMS

Consistent with theory, Kelly and St. Lawrence (1988) and Quadland and Shattls (1987) demonstrated that programs with both didactic and psychological components led to more pervasive and consistent change in sexual behavior. Although their programs varied in format, they incorporated psychological components similar to those that we have incorporated into our multifaceted program.

In Kelly's program, 51 experimental subjects who underwent training sessions reported substantially less high-risk behavior than the 53 control group members. At the follow-up, members of the treatment group eliminated high-risk sexual behavior almost entirely. Quadland and Shattls' group included men who had knowledge about the dangers of AIDS and who wanted to change their behavior, but had been unable to do so. In essence, they had defined themselves as having problems in sexual control. The groups run by Quadland and Shattls also showed a significant reduction in high-risk activity.

MENTAL HEALTH COUNSELING AND AIDS

The AIDS crisis elicits mental health and behavioral problems in a wide range of persons, many of whom do not have AIDS. Included are persons who engage in high-risk behaviors, uninfected persons with little chance of infection who over-react to the epidemic, HIV-positive but asymptomatic persons, and persons with AIDS and their families. This section focuses on alleviating the mental distress of HIV-infected persons or persons with ARC or AIDS and their families.

MENTAL HEALTH OF AIDS PATIENTS

When dealing with HIV-positive persons, psychotherapists should inquire about the physical, psychological, and social levels of each symptom. The disease has a psychological impact that is unique among terminal diseases because of the fear of infecting others, the long incubation period with concomitant uncertainty, and because of its association with gay and drug-abusing lifestyles. The complicated nature of the disease may require the psychotherapist to consult frequently with other health providers and members of the patient's family or social support systems.

Becoming HIV infected precipitates many mental health problems. Persons who acquire the infection must decide whether to continue in school, whether to pursue advances in work, and how much energy to invest in interpersonal relationships. In other words, they must make crucial decisions about the quality of their remaining life.

Other mental health challenges include facing their inevitable death from AIDS, and coping with depression, social isolation, suicidal ideation, neurological decompensation, and problems dealing with medical and other health service personnel. The problems are so severe that many patients with AIDS develop *DSM-III-R* diagnoses such as adjustment disorder with depressed mood, major depression, or anxiety disorder. The rate of premorbid psychopathology is unknown, but it appears that most of these disorders develop after patients learn that they have the HIV infection.

Counseling must be directed toward the unique needs of the patient. For some patients with limited time, counseling is not usually geared toward personality reconstruction. Instead, the goal of treatment is to assist the patient in enhancing the quality of life and facing death with courage, support, and dignity.

For other patients with a recent determination of HIV-positive status, it may be prudent to consider them as having a chronic disease. The chronic disease perspective may become more common as science develops more technology to prolong the lives of persons with HIV. For these patients the goal is to help them maintain their quality of life for as long as possible.

Life and Death Issues. The reactions of AIDS victims commonly follow those of persons terminally ill with other diseases; they include anger, denial, depression, and eventual resolution. Often persons with AIDS will lash out with extreme anger at the physicians who treat them, at other caregivers, or even at their psychotherapists. This anger may typically be viewed as part of the natural process of facing death.

The infected person may also threaten to infect others with the disease. Psychotherapists should evaluate this serious threat in the context of the death and dying reaction and should not necessarily take it at face value.

Denial often follows the anger. The denial of being seropositive is an attempt by the patient to ward off intense fears about dying. Intrusive thoughts or dreams of suffering and death may occur. These may be necessary stages toward the cognitive and affective integration of the event. Sometimes patients will re-experience the emotions surrounding the decision to become an active homosexual or to engage in high-risk behaviors.

When patients fully understand the terminal nature of the disease, feelings of anxiety, depression, and sense of loss are likely to develop. As part of this stage, persons with AIDS or HIV infection may become hypervigilant about any changes in skin tone, blotches, weight loss, fatigue, fevers, night sweats, swollen glands, or other symptoms. For example, a minor head cold may be regarded as the "beginning of the end."

When interviewing patients, regardless of which stages they are in, psychotherapists should avoid harsh confrontations, and should maintain a bias toward affective discharge and away from denial. Ideally, AIDS patients should learn to "live with AIDS" and accept their limited life span.

This realization will necessitate a major reorientation of the lifestyle and priorities of the patient. AIDS patients must often deal with pain and incapacity and adjust to changes in relationships with family, friends, and lovers. They will face decisions about alternative sexual practices, about how to tell friends and family, and about how to adjust to eventual decreases in income.

Patients may wish to make a decision concerning the use of extraordinary life-saving measures. Often patients decide against these extraordinary measures because they merely prolong pain and confusion. Such a decision relieves the patient's family members from having to address this issue. Spiritual advisors can help patients find meaning in their suffering and to look back on their lives with a sense of fulfillment and meaning.

Depression. Depression or melancholia is a natural reaction to learning that one has a fatal disease. The depression is likely to be characterized by a tremendous sense of loss as the person confronts loss of health, money, friends, and eventually life itself.

Some persons with AIDS experience prolonged depression and do not reconcile themselves to their life-endangered status. Many psychiatric referrals of AIDS patients are for depression, mostly adjustment disorders with depressed mood. Some persons will attempt to self-medicate by engaging in drug or alcohol abuse after learning that they are HIV positive.

The depression may be characterized by a sense of guilt for sexual or drug related behaviors. Western culture commonly links together sex, sinfulness, punishment, death, and damnation. Persons who are at some level uncomfortable with their gay lifestyle and who develop AIDS may believe, at least momentarily, that God is punishing them for their sexual behaviors. Reactions from family members and some religious leaders may reinforce this belief.

The diagnosis of depression needs to be made carefully, however, because the AIDS virus is also neurotropic as well as lymphotropic. Depression may mask early signs of neurological damage.

Psychotherapists who treat depressed persons with AIDS can use some of the same strategies that are used in treating depression in HIV-negative patients. Positive activities and positive social contacts can reduce melancholia. For HIV-positive patients who do not yet have AIDS, it is important to advocate a healthy lifestyle. Preliminary evidence suggests that HIV-positive persons who have healthy diets, engage in exercise, and avoid stress are able to reduce the effects of the HIV on the immune system and delay the onset of AIDS.

Pharmacological treatments for depression can also be used. Nothing about the HIV infection precludes the use of antidepressants, although the use of any medication requires consideration of the physical status of the patient and possible interactions with other drugs.

Social Isolation and Social Support. Social isolation is one of the major problems for patients with AIDS or HIV infection. Support systems are not always available. In some geographic areas, AIDS patients already have seen many of their friends die. Concurrent with the development of AIDS, then, these patients are simultaneously grieving for friends who have died. Such isolation and grief will increase the likelihood of depression.

Some gay or drug abusing patients will not have access to groups or persons who are sympathetic or uncritical of their condition. Gay and drug abusing lifestyles have inherent stresses, and many on the outside view them as inherently inferior. Instead of receiving support, some persons with the HIV infection or AIDS have faced a "social death" of ostracism by friends and family. For others, the public nature of their disease elicits discrimination, and they may be evicted from apartments or lose their jobs.

Developing new friends within high-risk communities is not always feasible. The gay community often shuns persons with the HIV infection, and other persons dying with AIDS cannot provide the reciprocity needed to develop friendships. Other persons with AIDS feel awkward because of disfigurement from skin blotches caused by Kaposi's Sarcoma or herpes sores, and from weight loss or other factors.

Furthermore, persons with AIDS or ARC often withdraw because the physical effects of fatigue, headache, and nausea make social interactions more difficult.

Telling loved ones about the infection may risk engendering even more loss. Intravenous drug abusers may be especially reluctant to share this information with their companions because they may lose their only social support. Similarly, gay men who disclose that they are HIV positive may risk losing their lovers.

Many persons with AIDS remain silent about their infection rather than risk rejection, until their physical illness makes it impossible for them to maintain a façade of normality. The loss of social support may be especially difficult for those who have not made their sexual preference public.

Biological family members react in different ways to being told about the infection. Some families reject the dying relative. Others rally around their loved one and provide support. Still, even those who try to be helpful often have mixed feelings toward the AIDS patient. Even families who reconcile themselves to the death of the loved one may believe that the syndrome is punishment for sin or misbehavior.

It is hard to underestimate the role of family and friends in providing social and emotional support to the AIDS patient. Family members and friends often play the decisive role in the maintenance of health and well-being of the patient. They help acquire access to medical and mental health services. Their support and concern is crucial in maintaining the quality of life until the person with AIDS dies.

Self-help or psychotherapy groups are an excellent resource for patients with AIDS as well as for their partners or families. Sometimes the groups separate persons with AIDS into groups according to the stage of the infection, with persons with early and advanced progression placed in separate groups. This grouping minimizes fearfulness that may arise when patients who are in early stages of infection interact with more seriously ill patients.

Effective groups accomplish more than just providing a forum for mutual complaining. In effective groups members both give and receive support. Also, groups can teach coping strategies for the common problems faced by patients and significant others.

In addition, many HIV-positive persons find a sense of community by donating time, money, and expertise to an AIDS support or advocacy group. Participation gives a sense of community and purpose as well as increased self-esteem. Access to AIDS advocacy groups also gives the patient access to up-to-date information on AIDS.

Social support can also come from friends; but if the person's lifestyle has focused on homosexual encounters, the change in sexual behavior may mean a change in social contacts. Persons whose social contacts had been dominated by sexual adventures will need to adjust to being restricted to nonsexual or safe-sex activities.

Neurological Disorders. AIDS Dementia Complex is the most common neurological complication of AIDS or ARC. Neurological and psychological effects can occur even before other signs of HIV infection appear. After the first signs of infection appear, it is hard to distinguish between the psychological reactions to AIDS and the organic problems caused by the infection. Psychotherapists must be vigilant for changes in a client's mood, speech, and motor control, and for cognitive deficits that could indicate the need for referral for a neuropsychological or neurological evaluation.

Between one-third and one-half of AIDS patients develop neurological symptoms at some point in their illness and one-seventh first present themselves for treatment with neurological complaints. These figures probably underestimate the presence of neurological abnormalities within AIDS patients. An unselected autopsy of 40 AIDS patients found that 75% evidenced abnormalities of the central nervous system.

The identification of cognitive deficits can be difficult because the symptoms may be subtle and mimic functional disorders caused by depression and anxiety. Language, memory, and integrative abilities are especially vulnerable to the cognitive decay. As the disease progresses, the severity and amount of neurological damage increases. Initial neurological examinations may be normal, and psychosocial explanations for the behavior may seem adequate.

Nevertheless, AIDS dementia should be suspected if depression occurs with cognitive deficits. This is especially important if the patient has no premorbid history of mental illness, shows soft neurological signs through testing, imbalance, tremor, or avoidance of hard tasks.

Medication may provide symptomatic relief for some patients. Zidovudine has been found to reverse AIDS dementia for some persons at least for some time. Also, psychostimulants such as methylphenidate or dextroamphetamines have been found to reduce cognitive or affective dysfunction. Evidence regarding the use of psychotropics or antidepressants is inconclusive. One study reported anecdotally that lorazepam decreased visual hallucinations and cognitive deficits with AIDS dementia patients.

The decline in cognitive ability has implications for the practice of psychotherapy. Therapy may have to adopt a "case management" approach to solving immediate problems as the patient's ability to handle abstract thought decreases. Themes in therapy should be kept simple.

Suicide. Persons with AIDS have suicide rates many times higher than the general population. AIDS patients have two periods of high risk for suicide. Shortly after the diagnosis is made, the suicide risk may be high due to the devastating psychological effects of an AIDS diagnosis. At that time patients feel panic, guilt, depression, and hopelessness.

Another high-risk suicide period occurs later in the course of the illness when health begins to deteriorate. The anxiety and the pain associated with the illness and medical treatments may exacerbate the depression. In addition, some persons with AIDS experience a biological depression caused by the HIV infection in the central nervous system. Some patients may have both psychological and neurologically based depression.

Suicide risk may be especially high for persons with a pre-infection history of mental disorders, who have sustained a recent loss of a lover or friend due to death, who have experienced social isolation after disclosure of their infectious status, and who have high levels of environmental stress.

Many patients who later committed suicide had expressed their intent to their doctors. Some had made previous attempts and were under current psychiatric treatment.

Dealing with Medical Personnel. The pragmatics of dealing with the physical aspects of the disease can be demanding because of anxiety surrounding the eventual deterioration in health. Understandably, persons who are HIV positive often fear that an ache or pain is the first symptom of AIDS. Even among persons with AIDS, it is estimated that about one-third of their symptoms are the result of somaticizing.

In addition, many patients have negative emotional reactions to their care providers. Some feel rage at the laboratory personnel who performed the tests. Others feel anger at their physicians and complain that they provided too much or too little information about the disease. Dependency needs increase, and relationships to authority figures such as medical personnel may be tested as feelings of helplessness arise.

The therapist has to decide which concerns are justified objectively and which reflect the irrational fears of the patient. Sometimes the anger is not just a reaction of the patient to the fatal syndrome. Sometimes physicians and other hospital personnel do act abruptly with the patient because of overwork or as a way of distancing themselves from the uncomfortable experience of someone else's death. In addition, health professionals are not immune from the irrational fears of AIDS that affect the public in general.

Pragmatic advice can help patients deal with medical service providers. Mental health problems may have a severe impact on the patients and render them incapable of complying with treatment regimens, causing their health to deteriorate more rapidly. Sometimes it helps to have someone go with them to the doctor's office so they can understand what is being said.

The patient may have to decide whether to participate in an experimental medication trial. These trials can increase the subjective sense of distress, and the very process of undergoing numerous medical procedures is inherently stressful. Anecdotal reports suggest that sometimes the researchers are more interested in the cell counts than the patient's sense of subjective well-being.

Nonetheless, some patients choose to participate in experimental procedures as a way of gaining a sense of purpose so that their suffering is not in vain. They may be able to perceive themselves as "soldiers" dying in the fight against AIDS.

A key treatment issue is whether to encourage the patient to maintain hope that current symptoms will subside or that new treatments may be forthcoming. It may seem incongruent at this time to talk about generating hope especially as scientists caution that any cure or vaccine for the illness may be decades away. Nevertheless, such efforts to engender hope are not Pollyannaish lies. The ability to maintain a hopeful atmosphere helps patients. The choice of fighting to stay alive should be kept open for them. A positive attitude and positive health behaviors can delay the decline of the immune system.

MENTAL HEALTH NEEDS OF FRIENDS AND FAMILY

The family members of an AIDS patient are likely to have mental health needs engendered by the illness. These are a legitimate concern in and of themselves, but also because the family and friends can help patients cope with the demands of the illness. Family, friends, and lovers often become severely depressed; they also may need assistance in combating the stigma associated with AIDS.

Even supportive families often feel ambivalence about the drug abusing or gay lifestyle. As noted above they may, at some level, perceive it as sinful and view the syndrome as punishment for the sin. Others may blame themselves for causing their child or friend to become gay or a drug addict.

Education is important for this group. The fact that they are offering support to a loved one does not necessarily mean that they understand how AIDS is transmitted or its natural progression.

Sexual partners also have fears of contracting the disease. Women of child-bearing age must consider the possible effects on children. Male lovers may be rejected by the family of origin as corrupting influences.

At times well-meaning friends or family may offend the patient if they do not allow the patient to retain as much autonomy as possible. Discretion is required in determining how much to intervene. Some patients with dementia or failing health cannot make basic decisions, but they should be allowed to do so as long as they are capable.

PROVIDER ISSUES

Those who work with AIDS patients have heavy demands placed on them. Providers often care for persons who are much younger and who will probably die before them. To carry on duties effectively, workers must first understand their own reactions or countertransference to persons with AIDS.

In addition, psychotherapists should keep abreast of developments in AIDS research. They must be informed about the biology, epidemiology, and legal aspects of AIDS. They must understand family and patient reactions. Psychotherapists must judge when to act as an advocate or mediator for the patient, when to let the natural support system do this, and when to let the patient act independently. Perhaps more than anything else, the psychotherapist needs to know when to draw on the expertise of others. Treatment of a multifaceted syndrome like AIDS requires the involvement of persons of many specialties.

Transference and Countertransference. Transference is used here in a broad sense to refer to the patient's reactions to the psychotherapist, and countertransference refers to the psychotherapist's reactions to the patient. Negative feelings that are not understood and resolved may interfere with the ability to conduct meaningful psychotherapy. The nature of AIDS makes transference and countertransference an especially important issue.

Patients may react to the psychotherapist with unwarranted acceptance or unwarranted rejection. Sometimes AIDS patients view psychotherapists as invulnerable, especially if they do not belong to one of the high-risk groups. On the other extreme, other AIDS patients who belong to a minority group with high-risk behaviors may expect condemnation or rejection and project it onto the psychotherapist.

The psychotherapist needs to deal with these issues openly to the extent that the patient is able to accept this approach. Psychotherapists can foster positive and healthy transference by emphasizing their commitment to making positive contributions to dealing with the AIDS epidemic. Psychotherapists who participate in community forums on AIDS, give professional presentations, conduct research, act as advocates in the political arena, or who address the AIDS epidemic in ways other than through direct psychotherapy, should make this known.

A positive attitude helps both the therapist and patient. This does not mean denying the reality of the fear, suffering, and inevitable death of the patient. Rather, it is based on the recognition of positive human values, such as concern for others, and courage in confrontation with death. A positive attitude can improve the quality of life and delay the deterioration of the immune system.

Countertransference issues also may interfere with psychotherapy. The most common countertransference issues involve fear of death or contagion, negative reactions to homosexuality and drug abuse, and ambivalence in working with terminally ill patients.

Working with AIDS patients may generate a fear of death from the contagion despite having been informed that there the fear has no rational basis. Although health care workers dealing with bodily fluids should take precautions, psychotherapists should have no reason for concern on this issue.

Related to the fear of contagion is the fear of death. The terminal nature of the disease reminds workers of their own vulnerability. Psychotherapists need to understand their own feelings about death and about working with the terminally ill. Individual death is an issue that all persons, including psychotherapists, have to face. This may be exacerbated in dealing with the death of a young person. There is an inevitable feeling of helplessness in the realization of one's impotence against death.

Reactions to Homosexuality. Some believe that effective psychotherapy with gay patients requires a "gay affirmative" attitude which values homosexuality and heterosexuality as equally normal or natural preferences. Furthermore, some hold that negative reactions of society can cause significant stress to gays and can exacerbate problems of guilt, shame, sexual dysfunction, or substance abuse. Anecdotal reports suggest that discrimination against gays and negative reactions to homosexuality have increased in recent years due to fear of AIDS.

Psychotherapists need to understand their reactions to AIDS patients or persons who have engaged in high-risk behavior. Although homosexuality is no longer considered a *DSM-III-R* disorder, many mental health professionals still do not accept it as a viable lifestyle. This nonacceptance can exist among those who consider themselves liberal, but who have had no contact with the gay lifestyle. Often psychotherapists have to ask themselves if some personal incident or prejudice makes involvement with gays difficult. If negative feelings are not understood, the psychotherapist may respond with detachment instead of empathy. There is a positive correlation between therapists' ability to empathize and their openness to countertransference feelings and ability to deal with them effectively.

Other Negative Feelings. AIDS victims activate a sense of helplessness in others which is difficult to acknowledge. Health providers may experience extreme anger because of feelings of helplessness and guilt. Angry feelings may also distance the therapist from the patient. The natural resistance to death can be experienced as anger toward those who have AIDS, and this can result in the patient's rejection of the therapist.

Overidentification. Not all countertransference problems have to do with undesirable feelings toward the patient. Extreme positive feelings toward the patient may reduce objectivity and overall ability to help the patient. Overidentification is likely to be present if the psychotherapist spends an inordinate amount of time with the patient to the point of ignoring personal needs and other professional responsibilities.

Support Groups for Providers. Studies have shown that support groups for persons working with patients tend to reduce their negative reactions toward these patients. Perhaps caregivers need this kind of support system in order to express their own feelings regarding this difficult work.

PEDIATRIC AIDS

Infants account for only 1% to 2% of the total number of cases of AIDS. This percentage is expected to increase rapidly as more women of child-bearing age acquire the HIV infection. By 1991, between 3,000 and 10,000 children are expected to have AIDS.

Most of the children with AIDS are born to drug abusers or women who have had sexual relations with drug abusers. It is anticipated that the increase of AIDS in the heterosexual population will be responsible for most of the increase in the number of children with AIDS.

Children usually acquire the infection through perinatal transmission as the HIV is transmitted through a mixture of the infected parent's blood supply with the fetus. A few children, however, acquire it through contact with infected blood during birth or through breast milk. The remainder of infected children acquired AIDS through contaminated blood products before screening of the blood supply for HIV started.

Most children born with AIDS die within 2 to 4 years. Although more recent aggressive treatments have extended the lives of these children, they survive in an institutionally dependent state. The younger the child is at the time the full infection establishes itself the greater the chance of morbidity. Stress and nutrition can also influence morbidity. Children appear to have a mortality rate similar to adults, but the clinical presentation differs. Children are more subject to recurrent and severe bacterial infections and salmonella. Conversely, Kaposi's Sarcoma is rare among children, but common in adult AIDS patients. Also, children tend to show severe neuropsychological deterioration such as delay in reaching developmental milestones and intellectual functioning.

PSYCHOLOGICAL AND NEUROLOGICAL ISSUES

The treatments for AIDS require frequent hospitalization and involve major psychological stresses and neurological changes in children. The lives of these children are often further complicated by the death of one or both of the parents, or the parents' limited ability to supply adequate care, due to the related diseases with which the parents themselves suffer. The stigma and social isolation associated with the AIDS infection further complicate the life of the child.

Some believe that the infection may produce subtle subclinical detrimental effects on cognitive functioning in children which may be among the earliest manifestations of AIDS encephalopathy. Neurological symptoms are as prevalent in children as in adults. Neurological findings in children include developmental delays, encephalopathy, seizures, or microcephalus. The medication AZT can, however, temporarily improve cognitive functioning and, in some children, reverse the neurological deterioration.

SCHOOL ATTENDANCE PROBLEMS

Older children face the problem of discrimination in schools and other public settings. Because of widespread fear concerning casual transmission of the virus, many teachers, parents, and other children react with unreasoned fear toward children with AIDS.

The legal status of children in school remains unclear, although some have argued that the Education for All Handicapped Children's Act or Section 504 of the Rehabilitation Act of 1973 prohibit discrimination because of AIDS or HIV infection. Mental health professionals should be conversant with the rapidly developing statutory and case law in this area.

National Guidelines. The CDC and the National Education Association have produced very similar guidelines on AIDS. They recommend that a team composed of a physician, public health personnel, the child's parent or guardian, and school personnel make the decision regarding the most appropriate education.

The CDC concluded that "for most infected school-aged children the benefits of an unrestricted setting would outweigh the risks of their acquiring potentially harmful infections in the setting . . . these children should be allowed to attend school" (CDC, 1985, p. 521). No medical grounds exist for excluding HIV-positive children from school, as long as they are healthy and not behaviorally disturbed. It may be prudent, however, to exclude the children for the sake of their own health when other children in the school have infections.

Children may be excluded if they lack control over body secretions (through soiling, for example) or if they bite or drool.

What Every Therapist Should Know About AIDS

Also, children who have oozing lesions that are not coverable should be placed in a more restrictive environment.

Kirkland and Ginter (1988) recommended that schools adopt procedures for handling AIDS-related issues even if students with AIDS are not currently in school. Given the rapid spread of AIDS into "middle America," many schools will be facing the prospect of having HIV-infected children enrolled. The establishment of guidelines in a dispassionate atmosphere will preclude an emotionally charged decision-making process later.

FEAR OF AIDS AS A CLINICAL SYMPTOM

Conscientious efforts by the federal and state governments and private organizations have increased public awareness of AIDS. This public service effort has reduced the spread of the infection, but it has increased the number of mental health patients with a fear of AIDS or a belief that they have AIDS. Some news services inadvertently encourage this fear by misrepresenting the possibility of casual transmission. In many cases, however, the patients' premorbid characteristics may contribute to their oversensitivity to stories about AIDS.

Various letters and comments have referred to patients who fear AIDS with labels such as "AIDS-phobia," "AIDSophobia," "pseudo-AIDS," "AIDS-panic," "AIDS-induced psychogenic states," "AIDS anxiety," "AIDS-paranoia," and "afrAIDS." In reality, these broad labels misrepresent the psychological processes involved because they conceptualize fear of AIDS as a specific fear, which it may not be. Although no systematic study has been done on patients who fear AIDS, published letters and case histories show that the fear of AIDS can be found in a wide range of psychiatric disorders. Furthermore, historical research shows that the fear of acquiring a life endangering disease is not a modern problem unique to AIDS.

PARALLELS WITH SYPHILOPHOBIA

Contemporary patients who fear AIDS are similar to patients who feared syphilis many years ago. MacAlpine (1957) reported that the fear of developing syphilis or other venereal diseases years ago gave rise to terms like "syphilophobia," "syphilomania," "venerophobia," "venereal disease phobia," and "venereal disease mania."

MacAlpine (1957) found that the fear of syphilis was associated with many kinds of mental disorders such as anxiety state, hysteria, hypochondriasis, depressive psychosis, melancholia, and paranoia.

He placed patients who feared syphilis on a continuum according to degree of reasonableness of their fear. The group at one end of the continuum had adequate reason to fear that they had contracted a venereal disease; a middle group had a venereal disease that was successfully treated, but now doubted that it had been cured; at the other end of the continuum were patients who had multiple somatic complaints that they attributed to syphilis, but had no adequate history of risk behavior.

Patients who fear AIDS can be classified according to the same continuum - except the AIDS continuum could contain no middle group that previously had the disease and was cured, because AIDS has no cure. Nevertheless, both continua show that the likelihood of infection is highest at one end of the continuum and the likelihood of severe psychopathology is highest at the other end.

THE IDENTIFICATION OF AIDS PHOBIA

In identifying fear of AIDS, the mental health practitioner should consider the reality of the fear as determined by a history of high-risk behavior and appropriate testing, and whether the fear of AIDS is a discrete symptom or one of several symptoms that would warrant a diagnosis of a major mental health disorder. Both features must be considered in determining the optimal diagnosis and treatment.

The Worried Well. Windgassen and Soni's (1987) report on 24 patients with a fear of AIDS found that almost half of the patients treated for fear of AIDS had no specific mental disorder and were successfully treated with supportive therapy and education. No further details were given about these persons, although they might have fallen into the category of the "worried well" described by Morin, Charles, and Malyon (1984). The "worried well" are persons who show no signs of psychopathology but who are appropriately worried about being infected because they have engaged in high-risk behaviors. They may interpret physical symptoms such as night sweats, fatigue, or appetite loss as the first symptoms of AIDS. The problems of the worried well are understandable because of the ambiguity in our understanding of the transmission and diagnosis of AIDS.

The psychological profile of the "worried well" of the AIDS epidemic today correspond to the "worried well" of the syphilis era years ago. In MacAlpine's (1957) experiences with the "worried well," the most emotionally healthy patients had a reasonable basis for their fear. The most emotionally disturbed patients lacked evidence for their fears.

The Pathoplastic AIDS Symptom. At the end of the continuum opposite the "worried well" are patients who strongly believe they have AIDS even in the absence of high-risk behaviors, or even in the face of having negative results on the ELISA or other tests for the HIV infection.

Windgassen and Soni (1987) found some fear-of-AIDS patients had obsessive compulsive disorders, depression, schizophrenia, and anxiety disorders. A review of other reports in the literature shows a similar divergence in diagnostic categories. Fear of AIDS has been found in conversion disorder, factitious AIDS or Munchausen's AIDS, generalized anxiety disorder, bipolar disorder, paranoid personality disorder, and schizoaffective disorder. Although ego-dystonic homosexuality is not a *DSM-III-R* diagnosis, some persons with fear of AIDS have been reported to be reacting to the ego-dystonic nature of their homosexuality.

Fear of AIDS has been further reported in patients with monosymptomatic hypochondriasis (atypical somatoform disorder) in which patients have a circumscribed delusion that their body parts are distorted. In this disorder the delusions are distinct from the rest of the personality and are not secondary to obsessions, depression, or schizophrenia delusions.

Other fear-of-AIDS patients have a major depression accompanied by overvalued ideas or delusions about AIDS. These overvalued ideas are similar to those found in severely depressed persons that are subject to cultural influences. The fear of AIDS sometimes reflects conflicts about intimacy or guilt for perceived past sins. These delusions leave as the patient responds to treatment.

The presence of a major mental disorder does not, however, exclude a rational basis of the original fear. Indeed, several of the patients mentioned above likely had engaged in unprotected anal sex with male partners while others had engaged in intermediate-risk behavior such as sexual relations with prostitutes.

PREDISPOSING FEATURES OF PATIENTS WHO FEAR AIDS

The clinical literature is too sparse to make solid generalizations about the premorbid state of severely mentally ill persons who present with an unrealistic fear of AIDS. Nevertheless, Harowski (1987) suggested that AIDS-induced anxiety may exacerbate pre-existing psychiatric illnesses. For example, mild dysphoria or social withdrawal may escalate into major depression or complete isolation. Oversensitivity or fastidiousness about cleanliness may escalate into paranoia or cleanliness obsessions. Other commentators claim that patients reporting fear of AIDS have premorbid tendencies towards obsessions, anxiety, or guilt about sex. Harowski's comments may be appropriate for the worried well, although other fear-of-AIDS patients probably represent the broad spectrum of all possible premorbid personalities.

Harowski also reported that men with high-risk behaviors without any psychiatric diagnosis may become worried or concerned about their health after seeing the effects of the epidemic among their friends. Evidence from other disorders suggests some validity for Harowski's suggestions. Siblings of children who died from childhood leukemia often developed a fear of contracting leukemia. Persons who fear cancer often are found to have had a relative or acquaintance who died of cancer. Patients with a fear of heart attacks had a nonsignificant trend toward having a family history of death by heart attack.

ASSESSMENT OF PATIENTS WHO FEAR AIDS

In assessing patients who fear AIDS the psychotherapist needs to consider two major factors: the presence of high-risk behaviors, and the presence of other symptoms of mental disorder.

Psychotherapists need to realize that infection with AIDS is a realistic possibility for patients who have engaged in high-risk behaviors. The psychotherapist should not assume that lethargy or appetite loss are evidence only of depression because these symptoms are also found in the early stages of AIDS. Although it is possible for obsessive and depressive patients (as for anyone else) to acquire AIDS through low-risk behaviors such as protected vaginal intercourse, the rumination about AIDS in the

What Every Therapist Should Know About AIDS

absence of high-risk behaviors suggests an overvalued idea and an unrealistic fear.

Often patients who fear AIDS will exaggerate the ease of AIDS transmission. One patient believed he acquired AIDS from a small cut from a barbed wire fence because an HIV-infected person had been injured in the proximity, although not by barbed wire. Another patient believed he acquired AIDS from superficial facial wounds after he was in a fight with an unknown assailant. Psychotherapists need to take careful histories because more disturbed patients may distort or misinterpret their exposures as a consequence of their psychopathology.

Diagnostic ambiguity can occur because the HIV infection cannot be identified until about 6 months or longer after the initial infection. Consequently, testing or repeat testing may be indicated for some patients. Nevertheless, exposing the patient to an additional expensive battery of tests in the absence of high-risk behaviors or symptoms of AIDS may compound the fear. Repeated testing long after the occurrence of the last high-risk behavior may also be countertherapeutic. Some patients with fixed ideas will conclude that the repeat testing is proof that the psychotherapist believes that they are really infected. But because AIDS can be a possibility for some patients, repeat testing may be used as an objective tool for carefully selected nonpsychotic patients.

The psychotherapist also needs to consider if the patient has a major mental disorder. Psychotherapists should make a standard mental status examination in the course of the interview to help determine the proper diagnosis. The fear of AIDS should not detract the psychotherapist from addressing other presenting symptoms. As noted above, physical symptoms may be misleading for the purposes of mental diagnosis because some of the early symptoms of depression, such as loss of appetite and lethargy, are similar to those found in AIDS.

In addition, psychotherapists can consider how the patient has responded to reassurances. If reassurance that tests have yielded negative results helps the person realistically appraise the likelihood of being infected, the fear probably resulted from inadequate information, rather than delusion. Although many patients who fear AIDS may find momentary relief after reassurance from a knowledgeable person, some will have a re-emergence of the fear a few days later with the same degree of intensity. A history of rejecting reassurances of the results of negative tests suggests a delusion or an overvalued idea.

Psychotherapists should also inquire whether the patient is experiencing guilt over sexual contacts that have occurred in the past. Guilt over an extramarital affair or relationships with a prostitute may precipitate concern about AIDS. In addition, social relationships can be greatly disturbed by the phobia. Some persons who fear AIDS avoid contact, even social contact, with family members to avoid contaminating them.

Finally, some patients who unnecessarily fear AIDS have a history of past concerns about other health problems. The description of the supposed infection is often given in detailed or dramatic fashion. The patient is not prepared to consider the importance of anxiety-triggering stimuli or to talk about feelings, attitudes, or the past experiences that appear to be the cause of the infection.

COMMENTS ON DIAGNOSTIC TERMINOLOGY

Psychotherapists should not use the term "AIDS-phobia" or similar terms because they are diagnostically misleading. The fear of AIDS is best seen as just one culturally relative manifestation of the patient's basic propensity toward fear and rumination. The fear of AIDS is one of several symptoms that need to be considered in making a proper diagnosis in a standardized framework such as that provided by *DSM-III-R*. The important characteristic is not the fear of AIDS but the mental process that keeps the patient from assessing danger realistically or acting upon that assessment.

STAFF REACTIONS TO AIDS

One of the psychological aspects of AIDS is the social discrimination that accompanies it. In part, the discrimination against persons with AIDS occurs because it is commonly found in homosexual or drug abusing groups who have experienced social discrimination. AIDS was once called "GRID," or "gay-related immune deficiency."

This discrimination has led to blatantly inappropriate actions such as police using rubber gloves when handling all homosexuals. There have also been reports of gays who have been expelled from taxis or restaurants, or denied jobs because they might have AIDS.

Fear of persons with AIDS is not restricted to flagrant acts of discrimination by laypersons. Reports have surfaced of health and mental health providers showing fear of persons with AIDS to such an extent that it affected the quality of patient care. Polan, Hellerstein, and Amchin (1985) reported that the psychiatric staff on an inpatient unit often showed fear of contagion, avoidance, or anger at patients with AIDS. Some staff distanced themselves by wearing gloves when they were not required. AIDS patients were not encouraged to participate in ward activities or to discuss their problems in group settings. Overall, the presence of AIDS patients caused treatment to shift away from a therapeutic milieu to individual treatment.

Other practitioners have found that staff who believed that AIDS could be transmitted through casual contact were more reluctant to have contact with the patients. These staff members appeared more anxious and had frequent ruminations about AIDS outside of work.

COMBATING IRRATIONAL FEARS OF STAFF

Special programs can help staff members adjust to AIDS patients. Simple didactic education can have some benefit. L. O'Donnell and C. O'Donnell (1987) found reduction in anxiety in participants who learned that AIDS could not be transmitted through changing bedpans or sharing eating utensils. Staff members who did not attend classes continued to have AIDS-related difficulties.

Amchin and Polan (1986) allowed their staff to express and discuss their concerns and feelings about AIDS and its victims in supportive individual interviews and staff meetings. In addition, ongoing educational programs increased staff knowledge about the disease and kept staff informed about new scientific advances related to the disease. At a 2-year follow-up, Amchin and Polan reported that the AIDS patients no longer presented a unique disruptive influence on the inpatient unit.

As the number of patients with AIDS or ARC increases, mental health staff will be called upon to treat them with increasing frequency. Staff reactions may vary according to factual knowledge about disease transmission and prejudice against homosexual or drug abusing groups.

Preventive education appears warranted, even in settings where AIDS cases are relatively infrequent. Discussions about factual knowledge and unrealistic fears in a supportive environment may minimize inappropriate reactions.

What Every Therapist Should Know About AIDS

IS THERE A DUTY TO WARN IDENTIFIABLE POTENTIAL VICTIMS?

Information about a patient's HIV status, like any information gathered in psychotherapy, must be handled discreetly. Unauthorized disclosure of HIV status could have severe repercussions for the patient including social ostracism and extreme embarrassment.

Nevertheless, psychotherapists often worry about conflict that may occur when they treat HIV-positive patients who have not told their sexual or drug-abuse partners about their infection. In this situation, does the psychotherapist have an obligation to warn the identifiable sexual partner?

Psychotherapists may incorrectly assume that men and women will be honest with each other about their sexual habits or infectious status. Kegeles, Catania, and Coates (1988) found that 12% of bisexual or homosexual men who obtained testing for the HIV said that they would not tell their primary sexual partners if they tested positive, and 27% said they would not contact their nonprimary partners. Almost one-fifth of the sample had been engaging in high-risk sex with nonprimary sexual partners.

Similarly, about 34% of sexually active single men reported they have lied about their past sexual behavior to women partners. In addition, 20% said they would lie about being infected with the AIDS virus (Elias, 1988).

To date, courts and state legislatures, with the exception of California, have not provided adequate direction on this issue. Many commentators, however, have claimed that the precedents from *Tarasoff v. Regents of the University of California* (1976) would apply here.

According to *Tarasoff*, confidentiality within psychotherapy is to be valued highly, but should never be absolute. Instead, the *Tarasoff* court stated that "the protective privilege ends where the public peril begins" (*Tarasoff*, p. 337). The *Tarasoff* court narrowly interpreted this exception to confidentiality and stated that:

> A therapist is not to be encouraged routinely to reveal such threats since such disclosures could seriously disrupt the patient's relationship with the therapist and with the person threatened. On the contrary, the therapist's obligations to the patient require that he not disclose a

confidence unless necessary to avert danger to others, and even then that he do so discreetly and in a fashion that preserves the privacy of the patient to the fullest extent compatible with the prevention of a threatened danger. (p. 337)

Tarasoff and other decisions regarding the duty to protect were based on longstanding precedents dealing with the duty of physicians to warn third persons about infectious diseases (e.g., *Simonson v. Swenson*, 1920; *Skillings v. Allen*, 1919). In both cases, courts held that physicians had an affirmative duty to act to protect others when they knew of patients who had infectious diseases or otherwise threatened to harm others. Consequently, the duty to warn with AIDS is not an extension of *Tarasoff*. Rather *Tarasoff* is an extension of a legal tradition dealing with the duty to warn third persons of infectious diseases.

Regardless of the legal precedents established by *Tarasoff* and other court decisions, an ethical responsibility to the public may necessitate a warning in certain situations. Even commentators who do not cite *Tarasoff* directly acknowledge an ethical responsibility to warn identifiable sexual partners of HIV-positive patients (American Psychiatric Association, 1988; Council on Ethics and Judicial Affairs of the American Medical Association, 1988).

The idea of breaking confidentiality with an HIV-positive patient is likely to be offensive to psychotherapists especially given the widespread social discrimination against persons who test HIV positive. This social discrimination warrants serious consideration by psychotherapists who have an obligation to respond to their patients with compassion and understanding.

ASCERTAINING THE DUTY TO PROTECT

The application of the duty to protect requires three factors: that the psychotherapist have a professional relationship with the patient, that there is an identifiable person in danger, and that the danger can be reasonably foreseen. Each of these three factors will be evaluated as they apply to HIV-positive patients.

Fiduciary Relationship. The first criterion simply holds that the patient must be in treatment with the psychotherapist. The psychotherapist-patient relationship is considered "special" and creates special responsibilities not found in ordinary social relationships. The other criteria are more difficult to establish or apply.

Identifiable Victim. *Tarasoff* and most subsequent cases have held that the duty to protect extends only to identifiable victims and not to all persons whom the patient could conceivably harm. Similarly, psychotherapists treating HIV-positive patients would only have to disclose the danger to identifiable sexual or drug abuse partners. This would most likely include spouses or lovers who live under an "illusion of monogamy" or an "illusion of exclusivity."

The duty to protect does not extend to casual sexual or drug partners unless they can be readily identified. The ethical question of warning casual sex partners is reduced because persons who engage in unsafe sexual activities or share needles presumably know the risks.

Foreseeability. The third criterion is that the danger must be foreseeable before the duty to protect can be invoked. Psychotherapists are not held responsible for warning of danger that cannot be foreseen. The issue of foreseeability creates the greatest problems with the duty to protect with HIV-positive patients because the research has not identified all the risk factors involved in HIV transmission. Although definitive guidelines for the psychotherapist are lacking, some broad guidelines can be formulated using the available information on transmission found in earlier sections.

HOW TO ASCERTAIN FORESEEABILITY

First, psychotherapists need to learn about the high-risk sexual or drug habits of the patient. If therapists fail to do so, they will have insufficient or inaccurate information to serve as a basis for conducting psychotherapy and for ascertaining the threat to others. Learning about the patient's current high-risk behaviors informs the psychotherapist of the degree of risks to others.

Second, the psychotherapist should encourage patients to obtain testing when they engage in high-risk behaviors. Many patients, as well as some psychotherapists, falsely assume that a single test can give an accurate diagnosis. As described earlier, the accurate identification of HIV status can involve three stages and could require testing 6 months to a year after the initial potential infection.

If the patient tests HIV positive, then the therapist needs to ascertain if the patient is continuing to engage in high-risk behaviors. Although the determination of foreseeable danger is difficult, its outermost boundaries are clear. Low-risk behaviors, such as occur by merely living together, definitely do not give rise to a duty to protect.

High-Risk Behaviors. If, however, the HIV infected patient is engaging in a high-risk behavior such as unprotected anal intercourse, the duty to protect would apply. In such a case the psychotherapist should try to persuade the patient to notify the sexual partner of the infection. If the patient fails to notify the partner, then it is conceivable that a court could hold a psychotherapist liable.

Unless the danger to the identifiable sexual partner is imminent, however, psychotherapists are encouraged to act cautiously and issue a warning only as a last resort. If the HIV-infected patient is engaging in protected anal intercourse or lower risk sexual behaviors, then the psychotherapist has more time in psychotherapy in which to persuade the patient to notify the partner (Knapp, VandeCreek, & Shapiro, in press).

Intermediate-Risk Behaviors. Perhaps the greatest difficulty in making the decision to warn comes with HIV-positive patients who engage in "safe sex" but who do not notify their partners of their infection. In this situation, the scientific experts might disagree about the degree of risk, and the legal authorities might disagree on the amount of risk required to justify a warning. An important fact here is that condoms do not provide absolute protection from AIDS. Dr. Michael Gottlieb, the physician who made the initial report of an AIDS patient in 1981, said that "there's no such thing as safe sex for someone contemplating sex with an HIV-positive person" (Goldsmith, 1988, p. 641).

We believe that the duty to protect should also apply to "intermediate"-risk behaviors such as protected intercourse. Although the risk of transmission is low, it still exists. Furthermore, the naive partner may view condom use as solely for pregnancy prevention and therefore may lack the incentive to be sure that condoms are used conscientiously. Although the risk of transmission is low (Hearst & Hulley, 1988, estimate 1 in 11 for

500 sexual encounters), the consequence of a failure is very high. "Even one failure is a failure for life" (Fineberg, 1988, p. 594).

When HIV Status Is Unknown. How should the psychotherapist respond when the patient is engaging in high-risk behavior or is sharing needles, but refuses to get tested or to learn the results of the test? Does a psychotherapist have a duty to warn in these circumstances?

Again, the available knowledge about HIV infection does not provide a precise equation to determine the degree of risk to the identifiable victim. The answer depends on the circumstances such as the number and frequency of high-risk sexual behaviors outside the marriage or stable relationship, frequency of sharing needles, the presence of other sexually transmitted diseases, and the prevalence of AIDS in the area.

In such cases the determination of danger requires two assumptions: that the patient is HIV positive and that the partner is at risk to acquire the infection. Because both assumptions can be difficult to prove, a duty to protect should not develop unless the patient is very likely to be or become HIV positive. The decision to protect should not turn into a "morality watch" where the remote threat of AIDS is an excuse to reveal extramarital affairs or intravenous drug abuse.

CLINICAL MANAGEMENT OF THE HIV DANGEROUS PATIENT

How should psychotherapists respond when dealing with HIV dangerous patients? The *Tarasoff* court said, "a therapist should not be encouraged routinely to reveal such threats ... unless such disclosures are necessary to avert danger to others" (p. 347). Neither the *Tarasoff* decision nor clinical judgment suggests indiscriminate reporting of the infection. A premature or inaccurate report of an HIV infection could damage both the patient's reputation and the treatment relationship. It would only deter people from seeking psychotherapy or cause those who are in psychotherapy to withhold information or terminate treatment prematurely.

Psychotherapists should always consider less intrusive means of diffusing the danger before making an exception to confidentiality. When sexual partners engage in "safe" sexual practices, the danger of infection is chronic and not acute. Psychotherapists have more time to persuade the patient to disclose the infection to a partner voluntarily. But, if the risk of transmission is high, psychotherapists should make the patient's voluntary disclosure of the HIV status a more immediate focus of therapy. Such patients present a more immediate threat of harm, and the necessity of confronting the danger issue becomes predominant.

Although no literature exists on how to encourage voluntary disclosure among HIV-positive persons, it is possible that literature dealing with the diffusion of aggression may be relevant (e.g., Appelbaum, 1985; Wexler, 1980). Efforts to improve the overall relationship between the couple may also eventually lead to a voluntary disclosure.

A few patients may claim that they will engage in sexual activity with the purpose of infecting others or without regard for the possibility of disease transmission. Nevertheless, the determination of immediate danger requires more than a verbal threat. This reaction may be a phase of dealing with the fatal nature of the disease and not represent a willful intention to harm others. Just as a verbal threat to assault a foreseeable third person may represent "blowing off steam," so the threat to infect others may reflect a momentary outburst of anger.

In making the final determination, the psychotherapist must often rely upon various subjective factors. The credibility of the patient, the perceived degree of concern for the identifiable sexual partner, the overall sense of social responsibility, and other factors must be considered.

Guidelines for Issuing Warnings. In some situations, however, resistive patients may give rise to the duty to protect. Clinical experience with potentially assaultive psychiatric patients provides guidelines when making the necessary disclosure. Potentially assaultive patients respond better when psychotherapists speak openly about their concerns for endangered third parties. Warnings should be made, if at all possible, with the patient's consent or with the patient present. The openness helps reduce the suspicion about what might have been said and may reduce the harm to the psychotherapeutic relationship. When psychotherapists have made the disclosure with the patient's knowledge or consent, patients may be more likely to continue in treatment (Beck, 1982). When psychotherapists issue a warning, they should provide the potential victim with additional information about HIV testing sites and sources of information about AIDS.

It is possible that a psychotherapist could seek the involuntary hospitalization of an HIV-positive patient who threatens others by his or her behavior. Of course, the basis for the commitment is not the HIV-positive status but a severe mental illness that creates the danger to others. Because of strict statutory guidelines for these laws, it is expected that psychotherapists would seldom use this option.

As with other dangerous patients it is important to document treatment decisions. Consultation with psychotherapist peers or physicians knowledgeable about sexual behavior, AIDS, or the HIV infection may be required.

Potential Statutory Remedies. Several states have enacted duty-to-protect statutes that limit the liability of psychotherapists who treat life endangering outpatients (Knapp et al., in press). These laws protect psychotherapists who make good-faith warnings when danger to identifiable victims is foreseeable. It is not clear, however, whether courts would apply these laws in instances in which the potential harm arises from HIV infection.

California has enacted a statute to guide health professionals who deal with potentially dangerous HIV-positive persons. This law provides immunity from civil and criminal liability for physicians or surgeons who disclose test results "to a person reasonably believed to be the spouse, or to a person reasonably believed to be a sexual partner or a person with whom the patient has shared the use of hypodermic needles or to the county health officer" (California Statutes, Health and Safety Codes, section 199.25 [a]). The law does not, however, permit the professional to give identifying information about the person believed to be infected. This law permits county health officials to notify threatened persons as well. The statute eliminates the *Tarasoff* doctrine in these cases by permitting, but not requiring, notification of potential victims. The permissive wording allows the professional to delay the warning while working with the patient to change sexual or drug behaviors or to make a voluntary disclosure.

The law also requires the physician or surgeon to first discuss the test results with the patient, give appropriate counseling and education about AIDS, and attempt to solicit voluntary disclosure. The potential victim must also be offered counseling and follow-up.

Several elements of this law correspond to the good clinical practices that we have suggested here, including counseling the patient, attempting to acquire voluntary disclosure first, and giving attention to the potentially threatened person. We would, of course, prefer to see psychologists and other psychotherapists included in this statute along with physicians.

SUMMARY

Most psychotherapists will eventually encounter the AIDS health crisis through their work with patients who are infected or through their work with family members, friends, or potential victims of AIDS patients. Other psychotherapists will be challenged by the AIDS crisis in their work as consultants with agencies who work with victims and their families or through participation in community educational efforts. None of us will remain unaffected.

Psychotherapists can play a vital role in this crisis. They can provide therapy and support to infected patients and significant others in their lives. They can help to educate the public about the parameters of the infection, and they can play a leadership role in designing, implementing, and evaluating programs that strive to change high-risk behaviors.

REFERENCES

Alberti, R. E., & Emmons, M. L. (1978). *Your Perfect Right*. San Luis Obispo, CA: Impact.
Allen, J., & Curran, J. (1988). Prevention of AIDS and HIV infection: Needs and priorities for epidemiologic research. *American Journal of Public Health, 78,* 381- 386.
Amchin, J., & Polan, H. (1986). A longitudinal account of staff adaptation to AIDS patients on a psychiatric unit. *Hospital and Community Psychiatry, 37,* 1235- 1238.
American Psychiatric Association. (1988). AIDS policy: Confidentiality and disclosure. *American Journal of Psychiatry, 145,* 541-542.
Appelbaum, P. (1985). Tarasoff and the clinician: Problems in fulfilling the duty to protect. *American Journal of Psychiatry, 142,* 425-429.
Baer, J., Holm, K., & Lewitter-Koehler, S. (1987). Challenges in developing an inpatient psychiatric program for patients with AIDS and ARC. *Hospital and Community Psychiatry, 38,* 1299-1303.
Barrows, P., & Halgin, R. (1988). Current issues in psychotherapy with gay men: Impact of the AIDS phenomenon. *Professional Psychology: Research and Practice, 19,* 395-402.
Beck, J. (1982). When the patient threatens violence: An empirical study of clinical practice after Tarasoff. *Bulletin of the American Academy of Psychiatry and the Law, 10,* 189-201.

Becker, M., & Joseph, J. (1988). AIDS and behavior change to reduce risk: A review. *American Journal of Public Health, 78,* 349-410.

Board of Trustees. (1987). Prevention and control of Acquired Immune Deficiency Syndrome: An interim report. *Journal of the American Medical Association, 258,* 2097-2103.

Bolling, D., & Voeller, B. (1987). AIDS and heterosexual anal intercourse [Letter to the editor]. *Journal of the American Medical Association, 258,* 474.

Brandt, A. (1988). AIDS in historical perspective: Four lessons from the history of sexually transmitted diseases. *American Journal of Public Health, 78,* 367-371.

California Statutes, Health and Safety Codes, Division 1.1, Chapter 1.20, section 199.95.

Can you rely on condoms? (1989, March). *Consumer Reports, 54,* 135-141.

Castro, K., Lifson, A., White, C., Bush, T., Chamberland, M., Lekatsas, A., & Jaffe, H. (1988). Investigations of AIDS patients with no previously identified risk factors. *Journal of the American Medical Association, 259,* 1338-1342.

Centers for Disease Control. (1985). Education and foster care of children infected with HTLV-III/LAV. *Morbidity and Mortality Weekly Report, 35,* 76-79.

Centers for Disease Control. (1988a). Condoms for prevention of sexually transmitted diseases. *Journal of the American Medical Association, 259,* 1925-1927.

Centers for Disease Control. (1988b). Guidelines for effective school health education to prevent the spread of AIDS. *Morbidity and Mortality Weekly Report, 37*(5-2), 1-14.

Centers for Disease Control. (1989). First 100,000 cases of Acquired Immunodeficiency Syndrome - United States. *Journal of the American Medical Association, 262,* 1453, 1456.

Chamberland, M., & Dondero, T. (1987). Heterosexually acquired infection with Human Immunodeficiency Virus (HIV). *Annals of Internal Medicine, 107,* 763-766.

Coates, T., Moran, S., & McKusick, L. (1987). Behavioral consequences of AIDS antibody testing among gay men [Letter to the editor]. *Journal of the American Medical Association, 258,* 1989.

Consortium for Retrovirus Serology Standardization. (1988). Serological diagnosis of Human Immunodeficiency Virus infection by Western blot testing. *Journal of the American Medical Association, 260,* 674-679.

Council on Ethical and Judicial Affairs of the American Medical Association. (1988). Ethical issues involved in the growing AIDS crisis. *Journal of the American Medical Association, 259,* 1360-1361.

Curran, J., Clark, M., & Gostin, L. (1987). AIDS: Legal and policy implications of the application of traditional disease control measures. *Law, Medicine, & Health Care, 15,* 27-35.

Curran, J., Jaffe, H., Hardy, A., Morgan, W. M., Selik, R., & Dondero, T. (1988). Epidemiology of HIV infection and AIDS in the United States. *Science, 239,* 610-616.

DiClemente, R. (1989). Prevention of HIV infection among adolescents. *AIDS: Education and Prevention, 1,* 70-79.

Education for All Handicapped Children's Act of 1975 (P.L. 94-142), *codified* at 20 U.S.C., §§1401-1461 (1978).

Elias, M. (1988, August 5). Many lie about AIDS risk. *USA Today,* p. D-1.

Ellis, A., & Harper, R. (1975). *A New Guide to Rational Living.* North Hollywood, CA: Wilshire.

Faulstich, M. (1987). Psychiatric aspects of AIDS. *American Journal of Psychiatry, 144,* 551-556.

Feldblum, P., & Fortney, J. (1988). Condoms, spermicides, and the transmission of the Human Immunodeficiency virus: A review of literature. *American Journal of Public Health, 78,* 52-53.

Fineberg, H. (1988). Education to prevent AIDS: Prospects and obstacles. *Science, 239,* 592-596.

Fischl, M., Dickinson, G., Scott, G., Klimas, N., Fletcher, M. A., & Parks, W. (1987). Evaluation of heterosexual partners, children, and household contacts of adults with AIDS. *Journal of the American Medical Association, 257,* 640-644.

Friedland, G., & Klein, R. (1987). Transmission of the human immunodeficiency virus. *New England Journal of Medicine, 317,* 1125-1135.

Gallo, R., & Montagnier, L. (1989). AIDS in 1988. *Scientific American, 259,* 40-51.

Gerbert, B., Maguire, B., Badner, V., Altman, D., & Stone, G. (1988). Why fear persists: Health care professionals and AIDS. *Journal of the American Medical Association, 260,* 3481-3483.

Goldsmith, M. (1988). Sex experts and medical scientists join forces against a common foe: AIDS. *Journal of the American Medical Association, 259,* 641-643.

Guerney, B. (1977). *Relationship Enhancement.* San Francisco: Jossey-Bass.

Harowski, K. (1987). The worried well: Maximizing coping in the face of AIDS. *Journal of Homosexuality, 14,* 299-306.

Hearst, N., & Hulley, S. (1988). Preventing the heterosexual spread of AIDS: Are we giving our patients the best advice? *Journal of the American Medical Association, 259,* 2428-2432.

Henry, K., Willenbring, K., & Crossley, K. (1988). Human immunodeficiency virus antibody testing. *Journal of the American Medical Association, 259,* 1819-1822.

Heyward, W., & Curran, J. (1988). The epidemiology of AIDS in the U.S. *Scientific American, 259,* 72-81.

HIV-related beliefs, knowledge, and behaviors among high school students. (1988). *Journal of the American Medical Association, 260,* 3567, 3570.

Kegeles, S., Catania, J., & Coates, T. (1988). Intentions to communicate positive HIV-antibody status to sex partners [Letter to the editor]. *Journal of the American Medical Association, 259,* 216-217.

Kelly, J., & St. Lawrence, J. (1988). *The AIDS Health Crisis.* New York: Plenum.

Kirkland, M., & Ginter, D. (1988). Acquired Immunodeficiency Syndrome in children: Medical, legal and school related issues. *School Psychology Review, 17,* 304-310.

Knapp, S., VandeCreek, L., & Shapiro, D. (in press). Statutory remedies to the "Duty to Protect:" A reconsideration. *Psychotherapy.*

MacAlpine, I. (1957). Syphilophobia: A psychiatric study. *British Journal of Venereal Disease, 31,* 92-99.

Morin, S., Charles, K., & Malyon, A. (1984). The psychological impact of AIDS on gay men. *American Psychologist, 39,* 1288-1293.

Number of sexual partners and potential risk of sexual exposure to Human Immunodeficiency Virus. (1988). *Journal of the American Medical Association, 260,* 2020-2021.

O'Donnell, L., & O'Donnell, C. (1987). Hospice workers and AIDS: Effects of in-service education on knowledge and perceived risks and stresses. *New York State Journal of Medicine, 87,* 278-280.

Osmond, D., Bacchetti, P., Chaisson, R., Kelly, T., Stempel, R., Carlson, J., & Moss, A. (1988). Time of exposure and risk of HIV infection in homosexual partners of men with AIDS. *American Journal of Public Health, 78,* 944-948.

Padian, N., Marquis, L., Francis, D., Anderson, R., Rutherford, G., O'Maley, P., & Winkelstein, W. (1987). Male-to-female transmission of Human Immunodeficiency Virus. *Journal of the American Medical Association, 258,* 788-790.
Partner notification for preventing Human Immunodeficiency Virus (HIV) infection--Colorado, Idaho, South Carolina, Virginia. (1988). *Journal of the American Medical Association, 260,* 613-615.
Perry, S., & Markowitz, J. (1986). Psychiatric interventions for AIDS-spectrum disorders. *Hospital and Community Psychiatry, 37,* 1001-1006.
Piot, P., Plummer, F., Mhalu, F., Lamboray, J.-L., Chin, J., & Mann, J. (1988). AIDS: An international perspective. *Science, 239,* 573-579.
Polan, H., & Amchin, J. (1987). Treating AIDS patients. *Hospital and Community Psychiatry, 38,* 531-532.
Polan, H. J., Hellerstein, D., & Amchin, J. (1985). Impact of AIDS related cases on an inpatient therapeutic milieu. *Hospital and Community Psychiatry, 36,* 173-176.
Potterat, J. (1987). Does syphilis facilitate sexual acquisition of HIV? [Letter to the editor]. *Journal of the American Medical Association, 258,* 473.
Quadland, M., & Shattls, W. (1987). AIDS, sexuality, and sexual control. *Journal of Homosexuality, 14,* 287-298.
Quinn, T., Mann, J., Curran, J., & Piot, P. (1986). AIDS in Africa: An epidemiologic paradigm. *Science, 234,* 955-963.
Redfield, R., & Burke, D. (1988). HIV infection: The clinical picture. *Scientific American, 259,* 90-98.
Rehabilitation Act of 1973, 29 U.S.C. 794 (1976).
Simonson v. Swenson, 177 N.W. 831 (1920).
Skillings v. Allen, 173 N.W. 663 (1919).
Stamm, W., Handsfield, H., Rompalo, A., Ashley, R., Roberts, P., & Corey, L. (1988). The association between genital ulcer disease and acquisition of HIV infection in homosexual men. *Journal of the American Medical Association, 260,* 1429-1433.
Tarasoff v. Regents of the University of California et al., 551 P.2d 334 (1976).
Valdiserri, R. (1988). The immediate challenge of health planning for AIDS: An organizational model. *Family Community Health, 10,* 33-48.
Valdiserri, R., Lyter, D., Kingsley, L., Leviton, L., Schofield, J., Huggins, J., Ho, M., & Rinaldo, C. (1987). The effect of

group education on improving attitudes about AIDS risk reduction. *New York State Journal of Medicine, 87,* 272-278.

Valdiserri, R., Lyter, D., Leviton, L., Stone, K., & Silvestre, A. (1987). Applying the criteria for the development of health promotion and education programs to AIDS risk reeducation programs for gay men. *Journal of Community Health, 12,* 199-212.

VandeCreek, L., & Knapp, S. (1989). *Tarasoff and Beyond: Legal and Clinical Considerations in the Treatment of Life-Endangering Patients.* Sarasota, FL: Professional Resources Exchange.

Wexler, D. (1980). Victimology and mental health law: An agenda. *Virginia Law Review, 66,* 681-711.

Windgassen, E., & Soni, S. (1987). AIDS panic [Letter to the editor]. *British Journal of Psychiatry, 150,* 126- 127.

OTHER TITLES IN THE PRACTITIONER'S RESOURCE SERIES

What Every Therapist Should Know About AIDS is one of eight books now available in the Practitioner's Resource Series. The other published titles are:

Clinical Guidelines for Involuntary Outpatient Treatment by J. Reid Meloy, Ansar Haroun, and Eugene F. Schiller.
    (IOTH) Paperback: $9.95   1990   78pp.
    ISBN #0-943158-45-1

Cognitive Therapy for Personality Disorders: A Schema Focused Approach by Jeffrey E. Young.
    (CTPDH) Paperback: $9.95   1990   90pp.
    ISBN #0-943158-46-X

Dealing with Anger Problems: Rational-Emotive Therapeutic Interventions by Windy Dryden.
    (DAPH) Paperback: $9.95   1990   62pp.
    ISBN #0-943158-59-1

Diagnosis and Treatment Selection for Anxiety Disorders by Samuel Knapp and Leon VandeCreek.
    (DTSH) Paperback: $9.95   1989   94pp.
    ISBN #0-943158-30-3

Neuropsychological Evaluation of Head Injury by Lawrence C. Hartlage.
    (NEHIH) Paperback: $9.95   1990   68pp.
    ISBN #0-943158-47-8

Pre-Employment Screening for Psychopathology: A Guide to Professional Practice by Rodney L. Lowman.
    (PESH) Paperback: $9.95   1989   86pp.
    ISBN #0-943158-34-6

Tarasoff and Beyond: Legal and Clinical Considerations in the Treatment of Life-Endangering Patients by Leon VandeCreek and Samuel Knapp.
    (TABH) Paperback: $9.95   1989   74pp.
    ISBN #0-943158-31-1

The following book will be available soon:

MMPI or MMPI-2? by Robert M. Gordon.
    (MM2H) Paperback: $9.95   Aug.1990   Approx.75pp.
    ISBN #0-943158-57-5

> **SHIPPING:** 8% ($1.50 minimum) in US. 15% ($6.00 minimum) Foreign and Canadian. Florida Residents: Add 7% Sales Tax.

If you would like to order or receive more information on any of these publications, please call (**813-366-7913**) or write (Professional Resource Exchange, Inc., P.O. Box 15560-H, Sarasota, FL 34277-1560), and we will be happy to send you our latest newsletter/catalog. When you call or write, please tell us your professional affiliation (e.g., Psychologist, Clinical Social Worker, Marriage and Family Therapist, Mental Health Counselor, School Psychologist, Psychiatrist, etc.) to be assured of receiving all appropriate mailings.

We are dedicated to providing you with applied resources and up-to-date information that you can immediately use in your practice. Our orders are usually shipped within 2 working days and come with a 15 day no-questions-asked money back guarantee.

Thanks for your interest!

Sincerely,

Lawrence G. Ritt

Lawrence G. Ritt, PhD
President